THE 'RULES OF THE GAME' OF SUPERPOWER MILITARY INTERVENTION IN THE THIRD WORLD 1975-1980

Neil Matheson

UNIVERSITY
PRESS OF
AMERICA

LANHAM • NEW YORK • LONDON

Copyright © 1982 by Neil Matheson

University Press of America,™ Inc.

4720 Boston Way
Lanham, MD 20706

3 Henrietta Street
London WC2E 8LU England

Library of Congress Cataloging in Publication Data

Matheson, Neil.
 The "rules of the game" of superpower military
intervention in the Third World, 1975–1980.

 Bibliography: p.
 1. Intervention (International law) 2. Soviet Union–
Foreign relations–Case studies. 3. Soviet Union–Foreign
relations United States. 4. United States–Foreign relations
–Soviet Union.. I. Title.
JX4481.M37   1982   341.5'8   81–43825
ISBN 0–8191–2495–8
ISBN 0–8191–2496–6 (pbk.)

72,928

ACKNOWLEDGEMENTS

Encouragement, sound advice and trenchant criticism on the part of the faculty of the Norman Paterson School of International Affairs at Carleton University, Ottawa, contributed significantly to the writing of this essay. Professors Theresa Rakowska-Harmstone, Douglas Anglin and John Sigler in particular are to be commended for this. The rigours of Oxford philosophy have made their mark thanks to the tutoring of Peter Hacker and Gordon Baker at St. John's College. The drafting of this work in Oxford and London during the summer of 1981 was rendered most enjoyable by the help and stimulation of friends and relations there, particularly Shean McConnell and the Rawcliffe/Nemet family. Finally, my parents are owed appreciation for their consistent support of a somewhat lengthy education.

N.C.M.

CONTENTS

PREFACE

This paper asks what, if any, were the "rules of the game" of superpower military intervention in the Third World. The rules are based on explicit or tacit agreements between the United States and the Soviet Union, or are inferred from patterns of mutual self-restraint. This continues the work of previous research by considering four cases: Angola (1975), Ethiopia (1977), Zaire (1977 and 1978), and Afghanistan (1979). The study covers international law, Soviet-American detente, the degree of one power's toleration of the other's interventions, spheres of influence, and the avoidance of direct superpower military confrontation. Rules did obtain in these cases, but based more on considerations of relative power than on shared conceptions of legitimacy.

The study was motivated by two considerations. First, the question "what were the rules of the game in this period?" had not been answered satisfactorily, despite frequent references to the concept both in the academic literature and obliquely in official, generally American, statements. Preconceptions or misconceptions about these may have important implications for subsequent foreign policy. A second and related point was the conviction that the study of human action devoid of considerations of intentions was barren if not meaningless. Intentions derive to some extent from Weltanschauungen which as in these cases can differ fundamentally. The futility of much of the detente controversy arose from failure or reluctance to appreciate this point. Conflict is not reducible to different perceptions, but the nature of any particular conflict is defined in part by these.

1. RULES AND INTERVENTION

This paper adopts a positive approach to the study of norms in conflict. This does not rest in seeking to evaluate conflict in ethical terms but rather in seeking to elucidate the nature of constraints set by rules about it. Statements about the content of the rules may deserve ethical evaluation, but this paper will not try to answer such questions although they will at least implicitly be raised.

The framework adopted is that of rules of the game as employed in the literature of international affairs. The type of conflict to be considered is that of American and Soviet military intervention in the Third World. Four instances of this will be examined: Angola (1975), Zaire (1977 and 1978), Ethiopia (1977), and Afghanistan (1979). The purpose of the essay is to discover what, if any, rules about military intervention obtained in these four cases, and whether these were respected or infringed.

The "Rules of the Game":

The concept of "rules of the game" refers to generalized prescriptions for international actors which on the basis of mutual agreement, either explicit or tacit, or on the basis of mutual restraint without any agreement, hold between the parties

concerned. The prescriptions concern expectations
of proper action, involving both normative evaluation
and prediction of such action. The actions may be of
a broad range or of a relatively specific type as in
this essay's concern with military intervention in
the Third World. There may be two or more actors
involved. These actors may be states, international
organizations, political parties, private corporations, the representatives of any of these, or any
other type of autonomous entity able and willing to
exercise influence with which international affairs
may be concerned. However, the term is usually
employed in relation to states and their representatives, and most frequently in relation to great
powers such as the United States and the Soviet Union.
This paper will follow this usage.

These prescriptions are not said to constitute
rules unless there is either agreement of some form
about them by the parties involved or they all follow
these rules without any such agreement on a reciprocal
basis. Cohen (1980) has provided the most compre-
hensive analysis of the basis of the norms, and his
classification will be employed.

(i)   International law may constitute a source of
       rules. Explicit rules are formulated either on
       the basis of custom or treaties. Customary law
       is binding on all states. Treaty law is bind-
       ing only on states parties and is the result of
       negotiation.

(ii)   Written accords resulting from negotiations
       which are not legally binding nevertheless
       create obligations between parties to them
       (Schachter 1977). There are no recourses to
       legal remedies in instances of violation of the
       agreement, but other parties are entitled to
       resort to appropriate sanctions in such cases.

(iii) Gentlemen's agreements are simply verbal promises
       exchanged between the representatives of the
       actors concerned. Obligations to respect such
       promises thereby arise.

(iv)   Parties to a written agreement, either legal or
       non-legal, may verbally or in a separate docu-
       ment reach a mutual understanding about it.
       This may involve merely a clarification of it
       or an extension or elaboration of the accord,
       so as to cover points which at its conclusion
       appeared to be obvious or had to be treated
       circumspectly.

(v)   Parties may arrive at tacit understandings of
       the rules. These need not involve negotiation
       but may involve either verbal or non-verbal
       signalling. Tacit understandings usually
       involve the making of claims in such a manner
       and their subsequent recognition by not being
       challenged. There can however be problems
       with interpreting a relationship as marked by
       tacit consent: action consistent with this
       does not necessarily imply acceptance or knowl-
       edge of such an agreement, and similarly
       infringement of such a rule may reflect igno-
       rance of it.

(vi)   It may be impossible to speak of either a tacit
       or an explicit agreement in circumstances
       nevertheless marked by certain behaviour by the
       actors concerned. A pattern of action may arise
       from mutual self-restraint whereby the parties
       limit their actions in similar ways on the
       basis of mutual expectations without even any
       signalling between them. Here it is also
       appropriate to speak of a rule, resting on
       reciprocity.

        A rule does not obtain unless at least one of
the above criteria are satisfied. These resemble
what Hart (1961:79) has termed rules of recognition,
which establish criteria for a rule to be a legal
norm. Rules of recognition constitute a type of
secondary rule of a legal system: these stipulate
how the primary rules concerning permissible and
impermissible action are to be recognized, changed and
adjudicated. Hart calls law a unified system of

primary and secondary rules. International law has
some secondary rules, albeit these are far weaker than
in municipal law. Features such as courts with
compulsory jurisdiction are generally lacking and
matters such as the interpretation of treaties depend
on the consent of states. International law is thus
in Coplin's words "quasi-authoritative" in resting on
this consent which is often not unanimous (1965:617).
Similar considerations apply to other types of rules
considered in this study: some level of agreement is
required although the rules may change and may not
apply to all international actors.

This range in types of rules including the
non-legal ones owes something to the McDougal-Lasswell
school of jurisprudence. This adopts a "policy-
oriented" approach to law, such that both legal,
political and moral norms are considered rather than
simply those written legal norms covered in a
positivist study of law (Moore 1974:3-37). Schachter
(1968:303) has noted that many scholars have recognised rules of the game other than international law
as constituting an "indeterminate" source of law.
Such an approach enjoys the virtue of comprehensive-
ness. It can also plunge into confusion or
incoherence when 'the law' is assimilated to other
authoritative means of decision-making to the extent
that no criteria for distinguishing between these
remain. The laudable aim of showing how non-legal
norms influence legal ones then is reduced to tauto-
logical proportions and in international law many
statements concerning lex ferenda parade as statements about lex lata. However a positivist view of
international law involving a logical distinction
between legal and non-legal norms can accommodate the
valuable contributions of the "policy-oriented"
approach. Reflecting this, international law is
considered as a separate category of rules of the
game although legal norms may grow out of non-legal
ones as discussed by Cohen (1980) and Bull (1977:67).

The value of employing this concept for this
study lies in assessing the role of rules of the game

4

in conflict. Deutsch (1973:378-381) ascribes two
functions to rules, those of regulating and of
resolving conflict. Rules constitute a necessary but
insufficient condition for the latter. A set of
rules by which an agreement may be structured may
include or overlap a set required for the regulation
of the conflict. Such rules may develop in the
course of negotiations and provide a framework for
these, as has been discussed by Zartmann (1975:71-74).
They may also be employed in tacit agreements not
involving negotiations. The rules may involve only
some of the parties in a conflict as the resolution
may not include them all.

In this paper concern is only with the role
of rules of the game in regulating conflict. Himes
(1980:18) has discussed how societies have norms which
prescribe the mix between conflict and co-operation
thus defining the limits to permissible conflict.
This institutionalization gives rise to a set of binding social norms involving collective social action to
endorse, regularize and reward permissible conflict
and to prevent recourse to impermissible action (212).
In relation to war, Howard (1979:14) has considered
how it is limited by both moral and prudential
considerations given that war is a social, purposive
activity. Yet more specifically, Cohen (1979:187)
has looked at threat perception as depending on
challenges to rules whose value lies both in providing
guides to prediction and restraints on conflict.

As rules generally involve agreement, they
require communication. Interesting studies of both
verbal (Franck and Weisband 1971) and non-verbal
(Cohen 1981) communication have been done. Such
signalling indicates the intention of the parties
concerned and so provides a basis for predicting
their actions. Miller (1977:58-62) has argued that
the desire for predictability is a prime motive in
agreeing to such rules. Albeit valuable areas for
study, such aspects of the rules will not be raised
but rather the focus will be on the nature of

permissible conflict held by parties as revealed in
the rules concerning intervention.

Recent literature on the subject has focussed
on Soviet-American relations. Such studies have
covered the principles of restraint possible (Bull
1977:207) or operative in crises (Holbraad 1979:109),
the basis of obligation of the rules (Schachter 1978:
305), the nature of each power's zone of influence
(Vazquez 1973) and its attendant rules (Schwarzenberger
1959) and the rules compatible with detente
(Schwarzenberger 1981). This study will continue this
work in the field of Soviet and American military
interventions in the Third World.

The Concept of Intervention:

"Intervention" means the organized and
systematic use of coercion by one state or non-state
actor in order to change or prevent change in the
political structure of another state or in its
internal or external policies, action or capabilities.
As a coercive activity, it is thus distinguished from
influence or non-coercive interaction: without such a
distinction the concept is meaningless given the
degree of interaction between actors in international
affairs. The type of coercion involved does not
matter: it may be economic, military or diplomatic.
Threats to intervene, although significant in their
effect, are logically distinct and do not count as
intervention.

Talleyrand argued that intervention and non-
intervention were indistinguishable, as both contributed to the outcome of local conflicts (Modelski
1961:9). However to drop the distinction is to render
the concept useless, as in any given situation all
states or other actors would be intervening and the
concept will be applicable to any action or inaction.
The concept is only of value if it discriminates some

types of events from others. This is not to deny that non-intervention may have important effects in a local conflict, nor that it may either be justified or unjustified. But not to intervene in a given situation differs from intervention which involves coercive action.

Although jurists such as Lauterpacht (1947: 19-23) have defined intervention as illegal, this study will profit from excluding such a consideration in the definition so as to leave open the question of legality to further study. Therefore it is assumed that intervention may occur with the consent of the recognised government, contra Thomas and Thomas (1956:71), and without "amounting to a denial of the independence of the state", contra Lauterpacht (1947: 19). Intervention in this case is still coercive as it may involve using force against the internal or external opponents of the government. Similarly it is not assumed that intervention either is or is not justified on other grounds. This then obviates the need for moves such as the Soviet one of condemning all interventions while denying that socialist states are capable of intervening. The question of justification will not be settled by calling one state's intervention another state's fraternal aid.

Rosenau (1968) has given a widely-cited definition of intervention, the three main points of which are weak. First, he holds that it is "convention breaking" and is not part of the normal pattern of interaction between states. This begs the question of what constitutes the conventional type of interaction. Some case can be made for there being conventions of intervention between the US and Latin American states and between the USSR and East European states. Zaire, formerly the Congo, has had a post-colonial history marked by several military interventions: is this conventional or unconventional? Indeed the entire point of this paper is to consider what conventions apply in instances of intervention.

Second, while Rosenau describes intervention well as being directed to the "authority structure of the target society", he misses possible degrees of intervention by excluding from this the internal or external policies or capabilities of such societies. Cases of military intervention generally are directed at the decision-making process rather than at individual decisions, but other forms of coercion, such as economic sanctions, may be aimed only at particular policies or capabilities.

Third, Rosenau claims as a virtue that his concept of intervention does not require an assessment of the intervener's motivation which he holds to be virtually impossible to ascertain. It is not clear whether his scepticism stems from epistemological convictions or political cynicism. The former is incoherent while the latter taken to such lengths is unjustified. The following paper is largely concerned with the ascriptions of intention and interpretation of actions in light of these. Like any field of human action, international politics does not lend itself to totally unambiguous interpretation. The search for the best possible interpretation requires among other things consideration of the evaluations presented by the actors concerned. Such statements are necessarily good, albeit defeasible, evidence for their intentions. In the light of further evidence not at present available, such as state papers or personal memoirs, the conclusions reached below may be overturned. But this does not create grounds for scepticism of a general nature but rather shows the possibilities, albeit within the limitations of evidence, for the ascription of intentions to actors.

A further feature of definitions held by Young (1968) and Schwarz (1970:32) is that the intervening state is stronger than the target state. There can be little reason for this. Albeit contrary cases may be rare, there is no gain in excluding these simply on definitional grounds. This would also lead to difficult questions: although Somalia intervened in Ethiopian affairs in the Ogaden war in 1977-1978, was it obviously the more powerful country even in

8

military terms? Such a feature will therefore not be included in the definition.

Evron (1979:19) has further noted that "intervention" is to be distinguished from "crisis". Following Brecher's definition of the latter, he argues that surprise, perceived threat to vital interests and a short time span for a response to this threat are not necessary features of an intervention. Particularly with military interventions, there is a high expectation of violence and this indicates the connection between interventions and crises. In the four cases under consideration, it is arguable that none constituted a crisis so defined.

As a coercive activity, intervention can take many forms. It may be political or diplomatic, economic, or military. The latter will be the only one considered in this paper. This is not to deny that the other forms are not of interest: indeed it is often alleged that economic intervention is prevalent in relations between the West and the Third World. It would also be valuable to examine the relationship between different types of intervention. But these issues go beyond the scope of this work.

Military intervention can be distinguished by two broad types, which will be called indirect and direct. Indirect intervention involves the supply of arms and related military material such as transport as well as training personnel for this equipment to a party to a conflict: essentially it involves providing that party with the instruments of coercion for its own use. This would include funding the group so that it could obtain weapons and supplies from another source. Providing a sanctuary for such troops or guerillas outside of their country of operations would be a borderline case of military intervention: there may be no provision of the instruments of coercion unless food is included under this heading but this aid may be relevant in enabling the forces concerned to operate militarily.

Direct intervention involves the introduction
of either the regular military units of the intervening state into the conflict or those of an ally or
proxy. Thus the intervener can be an agent of
coercion. Such units may be involved in "shows of
force", transport or other logistical roles, actions
to deter other potential interveners short of the use
of force, or actual combat. In the case of employing
an ally or proxy, the intervening state furthers its
aims in relation to the target state by giving these
units political, economic or military support.

Each of the cases studied involves both direct
and indirect intervention. The latter always preceded
the former, and the two types tended to be seen as
separate stages, although the transition from one to
another might not be clear-cut. The interventions
also varied in scale--in terms of amounts of arms or
material, number of troops and size of transport or
other supporting military units--and in duration.
Distinguishing specific interventions from the regular
supply of arms and the long-term stationing of forces
in another state is important in order to focus on
sufficiently discreet events that comparisons for the
purpose of this paper may be made. This can be done
by considering the purposes of intervention: in the
cases to be considered they were either to forestall
or to promote change in the political structure of the
target state in response to relatively specific
threats to that structure or opportunities for change.

Intervention in the Third World:

The "Third World" is a notoriously vague
concept but two sets of criteria are applicable in
the context of this study. One involves a low level
of economic development. Another involves exclusion
from the Western and Soviet blocs as traditionally
described. As the concern is with intervention, cases
such as Czechoslovakia and the Dominican Republic

would be comparable and have been the subject of such a study (Franck and Weisband 1971). If Latin America is considered to lie within the American sphere of influence and Vietnam within the Socialist Commonwealth, for the purposes of a study of intervention it may be unclear whether to include them within the Third World. The cases studied in this paper fulfil both sets of criteria and avoid such difficulties.

The Angolan interventions by the USSR and the US were aimed to back their respective preferred liberation groups in the country: the Movimento Popular de Libertação de Angola (MPLA) for the Soviets, and the Frente Nacional de Libertação de Angola (FNLA) and the União Nacional para a Independencia Total de Angola (UNITA) for the Americans. This arose in the aftermath of the April 1974 coup in Portugal when that country decided to abandon its African colonies. The transitional coalition government formed in January 1975 dissolved in factional fighting in the spring, with each side receiving ever-increasing, but ultimately unequal, levels of military support from abroad.

The Soviet Union intervened both directly and indirectly. The latter marked its involvement from October 1974 when it resumed arms shipments via Dar-es-Salaam and the Congo (Brazzaville) to the MPLA. This increased in the March-June 1975 period and by October was estimated to have been 27 shiploads of military equipment and 30 to 40 air supply missions. By March 1976 the US estimated the total value of Soviet supplies at $200 million and the number of Soviet military advisers was approximately 400. In terms of direct intervention, Soviet air and naval units were involved in the transport of Cuban combat troops to Angola from at least November onwards. Cuban units arrived as early as late September, initially without Soviet transport. However the main dispatch of Cuban forces, from November 1975 to March 1976, required substantial Soviet logistical support. By the end of that period the Cubans numbered 12,000. They are still based in Angola, numbering 21,000 in May 1978.

The American intervention was indirect, involving arms supplies via two routes. The CIA launched a covert operation in July 1975, with Forty Committee approval for $14 million worth of equipment to the FNLA and UNITA. A further $32 million was requested in November, by which time the House Select Committee on Intelligence stated that $31 million of supplies had been sent on CIA estimates, but that this had been undercosted substantially. Arms credits were also sought for Zaire, with $79 million requested in November, so as to channel arms to the FNLA and UNITA this way. The Ford Administration's requests were not approved by Congress. However, the value of American support sent to Angola via both routes is estimated at up to $80 million in the period up to November 1975 (Bender 1978:86-89).

The US might have been more directly involved via proxies or allies, but in both cases evidence is insufficient to demonstrate the extent of the involvement. Zairean troops were deployed in Angola alongside the FNLA but it is not clear at what strength or for how long. Zaire certainly did receive American political, economic and military support at this time. The South African intervention is better documented (Hallet 1979). Following "hot pursuits" of the South West Africa People's Organization (SWAPO) and limited operations in southern Angola, two columns entered Angola on October 19, 1975 to press back the MPLA forces. These were led by South African officers and supported by SA armoured cars, although consisting mostly of FNLA troops and Portuguese colons. On November 15 a regular SA unit of 1,000 to 1,500 men followed: South Africa did not commit more than 2,000 men to the fighting. Given intelligence and military ties between the US and SA the former may have known about the intervention beforehand (Hallet 1979:362). However there is no evidence of collusion on any level despite their common aim of opposing the Soviet-Cuban intervention. The United States did not even support South Africa diplomatically, as Pretoria learned to its loss. The case for American intervention in this sense is unsubstantiated.

In Ethiopia, the Soviet Union acted so as to support the Derg in its struggle to retain control over Eritrea and the Ogaden. Indirect intervention included an arms agreement for $100 million in December 1976, although apparently little of this was delivered. Mengistu concluded another one valued at $400 million in May 1977, deliveries of which were made by September. An estimated $1 billion worth of equipment was delivered by February 1978, including 450 tanks, 200 armoured personnel carriers, 30 artillery pieces and 50 fighter aircraft. Some 1,000 Soviet advisers and trainers were in Ethiopia by January. In terms of direct intervention, the Soviet air force employed 225 transports between December 1977 and January 1978. Twenty naval warships were deployed off the Horn of Africa, some of which bombarded Massawa when held by the Eritrean secessionists. Three brigades of Cuban troops, numbering 10-11,000 by March 1978, as well as 2,000 South Yemeni soldiers, were brought into Ethiopia. As in Angola, the Cuban troops have not yet left.

In Shaba I and II the US reacted to what it perceived as a threat to Zaire's Mobutu in the attack on that province by forces of the Front de Libération National du Congo (FLNC) in March 1977 and May 1978 respectively. The American reaction in the first instance was to only send $13 million of "nonlethal" military equipment and spare parts: Mobutu's request for tanks and arms was refused. The United States denied foreknowledge of the intervention of 1,500 Moroccan troops flown in 11 French transports, and denied having encouraged it. The American involvement in Shaba II was somewhat greater. In indirect terms, $17.5 million of fuel, equipment and medicine was sent to Zaire. In direct terms, American C-141 transports flew the Belgian and later the African troops into Shaba. The 02nd Airborne Division was placed on alert but never employed. The US unambiguously supported this intervention politically. Six hundred French, 1,750 Belgians and 2,700 African soldiers were involved in an operation lasting two months.

13

The Soviet Union intervened in Afghanistan in two stages of concern to its client the People's Democratic Party of Afghanistan (PDPA). Both involved supporting it against widespread insurgency and the second also involved a coup internal to the PDPA. From April 1978 at its assumption of the government, to December 1979 when Amin was overthrown, the PDPA received Soviet military supplies which included 30 Mi-24 helicopters, 800 tanks, and 800 armoured personnel carriers as well as fighter aircraft. There were also 1,500 advisers in Afghanistan by the end of 1979. Soviet troop deployments in Afghanistan began in July with a motorized infantry division according to John Erikson's testimony before the Commons Foreign Affairs Committee (Lange 1981:75-77). In November twenty battalions were placed to defend Soviet installations. For the December coup 4-5,000 troops were airlifted into Kabul followed by the advance of 50,000 troops across the Soviet-Afghan border. By February 1980 there were 70,000 Soviet soldiers in Afghanistan and a further 30,000 on its border. By the end of 1980 85-100,000 Soviets were deployed within the country, and they continue to be engaged in combat.

Although these interventions will be treated comparatively, this is not to ignore substantial differences in scale and duration between them. In particular, the US has been far less active as an intervener in this period than has the Soviet Union. One clearly cannot speak of a rule of _mutual_ self-restraint regarding the size and duration of these interventions. Such differences are an important consideration: the rules will depend to some extent on the nature of the game at any one time. The period of this study differs from previous ones and may do so from subsequent ones. The rules may change correspondingly.

Considerable research has been done on Third World military interventions. Some of this has involved considerations of the rules of the game of these interventions. Falk (1980) and Kahler (1979) have warned that these could lead to infringements or misunderstandings concerning the rules and so provoke counter-intervention and increase the risk of a Soviet-American war. This would constitute an instance of threat perception being linked to the rules of the game as considered by Cohen (1979:187). Such rules in the Third World have been considered by Hassner (1977:21), McConnell (1979:240), Zagoria (1979), Legvold (1979), Ayoob (1979), Evron (1979) and Sella (1981:21). The following framework is based to some extent on their work.

This paper will consider what, if any, were the rules of the game of military intervention in the Third World held by the United States and the Soviet Union, and whether those rules were infringed or not. The following areas will be studied to answer these questions.

(i)   International law: Did the two states agree on the nature of the legal obligations concerning intervention binding on them? Did they respect these obligations?

(ii)   Soviet-American detente: Did the United States and the Soviet Union agree on a code of detente regarding military intervention in the Third World? If there was such an agreement, did the two states respect it?

(iii)   Status quo: Were there any agreements on how the two should react to political change in the Third World?

(iv)   Spheres of influence: Did the two states reach any tacit understandings regarding spheres of influence in the Third World?

(v)   Military confrontations: Were there any tacit understandings or simply consistent patterns of restraint such that each state reduced the risk of a direct military confrontation with the other?

There is a certain degree of overlap between these areas. Soviet interpretations of international law involve assessments which will be considered under detente and spheres of influence. The Soviet and American conceptions of detente are based on their respective understandings of the correlation of forces and the balance of power, and these are considered as well under the status quo heading. But although these rules and their interpretations are interrelated, this does not mean that they are indistinguishable. They will then be rendered as separate as possible so as to formulate them with as much clarity as possible.

2.   INTERNATIONAL LAW

Although international law is not included by many authors in their consideration of rules of the game, it does constitute a source of such rules as defined above. Legal arguments have been prominent in the diplomatic battles waged over these interventions. In keeping within the rules of the game framework, the arguments employed by the US and the USSR will be evaluated to discover what, if any, rules arose on the basis of agreement.

Such an approach is insufficient as a piece of legal scholarship, focussing on states which with or without justification intervene in the affairs of other states. However this approach has the virtue of determining state practice in these cases. This may or may not conform to other statements of the norms regarding intervention as given in bilateral or multilateral treaties, in the resolutions of international organizations, by other states or by legal scholars. This then does not pretend to provide a definitive exposition of the law concerning intervention--assuming that one can speak of the law or set of laws recognized by all states. However the claims of the US and the USSR will be gauged according to criteria which are reasonably clear to determine whether the practice of these states follows the rules which they are alleged to follow.

Soviet interpretation of international law in particular is characterized by conceptions not widely shared, at least not outside of the socialist bloc. Following Marx, law is but a superstructural element which is determined by the economic base. Following Lenin, law is a weapon in the class struggle to further the aims of the proletariat and to be used by its embodiment in the vanguard party and by extension by the socialist state. However Soviet attitudes towards international law have gradually moved away from opposition to it as a creation of capitalism to an acceptance of it and willingness to work within its framework (Mitchell and Leonhard 1976). Assessments regarding the "progressive forces" may weigh heavily in decisions such as the recognition of the government in a civil war, but similar considerations can also feature in American recognition of "anti-communist" or "moderate" groups. It is only in exceptional cases, such as Czechoslovakia in 1968, that previously-held legal rules have been overwhelmed by class-based considerations and associated rules. Even in Afghanistan, the Soviet Union presented legal justifications which were logically distinct from class-based ones and were not supported by the latter. The two types of justification will therefore be considered separately, albeit they are deployed simultaneously.

Given the weakness or non-existence of what Hart has termed secondary rules as discussed above, international law depends on the consent of states on matters of interpretation. The unanimous vote for the UN General Assembly resolution in 1965 condemning intervention (A/Res. 2225/(XX)-App. 2) misleadingly suggests agreement among states about it. Younger has described the norm as one "in disarray", noting that the US voted for the resolution despite the fact that many states viewed it as at least an oblique condemnation of American intervention in Vietnam (1970:18). The resolution does not admit of any exceptions to non-intervention, yet state practice has at least claimed the legality of several types of exceptions.

Friedmann has considered several conditions for these (1970:57-64). They include the consent of

the government, attack on the target of intervention
by a third state, threats to nationals, humanitarian
suffering, self-determination and civil war. Jurists
view all of these as controversial. Whatever the
merit of their arguments, these will not be considered
except to illustrate points of interest in the cases.

Four lines of argument were employed. Intervention was justified in all four cases as having the
consent of the government of the target state and as
countering aggression against that state. In one
case, the threat to nationals was cited as a circum-
stance justifying intervention, and in another the
struggle against colonialism. The questions to be
answered are: what were the legal norms concerning
military intervention held by the US and the USSR, and
were they respected?

Consent of the Government:

The United States and the Soviet Union have
both stated publicly that the consent of the government of the target state is required in order for
military intervention to be legal. However while
agreeing on the rule and respecting it in Ethiopia and
Zaire, it was clearly broken in Afghanistan and in
Angola, albeit the latter case was complicated by
being a civil war.

Angola illustrated an often-discussed problem
in the international law of intervention. Given that
recognition is at the discretion of states, different
factions fighting for power in a civil war may be
recognized by different states and thus both sides may
claim the outside support that they receive to be
legitimate. The result is effectively a breakdown in
the norm of non-intervention and a mockery of the rule
that in a civil war either only the government may be
supported or neutrality must be observed.

The Soviet Union argued that the support sent
to the MPLA in the form of arms and troops went at the
request of the legitimate government of Angola. This
government was declared in Luanda on November 11, 1975
and recognised by member states of the socialist bloc
and former Portuguese colonies including Brazil. The
rival government of Roberto and Savimbi declared the
same day in Huambo received no de jure recognition.
The Ford Administration denied that the MPLA was the
legitimate government and insisted that only one
established according to the Alvor and subsequent
agreements would so qualify. The Soviet-Cuban intervention was said to be imposing a government on Angola
(Senate 1976a:8-11,174).

The Soviet position was subsequently vindicated
by the OAU's recognition of the MPLA in February 1976,
followed by several Western European states. The UN
Security Council Resolution 387 of March 31, 1976
(App. 5) reaffirmed the right of every state to
request assistance from abroad and in condemning only
the South African intervention implicitly accepted the
Soviet argument.

Despite these facts, the Soviet argument was
faulted. First, their support to the MPLA preceded
de jure recognition of it. Cuban troops arrived in
September 1975 and these cannot have done so at the
request of an MPLA government. Second, their recognition of the MPLA was inconsistent with earlier
declared support for the Alvor agreement of January
1975, and Nakuru one of June 21, both of which called
for a coalition government to succeed Portuguese
colonial rule, and the OAU decision of August 1 at
Kampala (AHG/Res. 72/(XII)-App. 8) which requested a
ceasefire and negotiations between the three parties.
This disregard for the rule concerning consent was
evident in the Soviet attempt to convince Amin, the
Chairman of the OAU, to recognise the Luanda government.

Third, the intervention of Soviet-backed Cuban troops into the conflict reversed the MPLA's military setbacks of October 1975, and enabled it to gain de facto control over most of the country by February 1976. Recognition of the MPLA by other states on the basis of this control thus provided a post facto justification for the intervention.

Fourth, the OAU and UN reactions which supported the Soviet position did so on the basis of objecting to the South African intervention rather than on the merits of the MPLA case. Amin protested to Roberto and Savimbi that support from South Africa could lead an OAU majority to reconsider its backing for a coalition government. Nigeria was one of the key states in changing the OAU decision and it singled out the South African intervention in explaining its recognition of the MPLA. The post facto Soviet legitimacy was primarily due to South Africa's intervention and to Soviet and Cuban determination to back their client militarily and diplomatically.

Although the US did not directly intervene in Angola, it also arguably broke its own professed support for the coalition government. The United States favoured Holden Roberto's FNLA, and although not counting as military intervention, his $10,000 a year retainer was raised to $300,000 in January 1975, which allowed him to purchase a radio station and A Provincia de Angola, the country's largest newspaper. This was not obviously consistent with public backing of the Alvor agreement. The indirect military intervention which was authorised in July enabled the FNLA and UNITA to buy arms. Kissinger argued that this was required in the face of Soviet military supplies to the MPLA (Senate 1976a:10). But the Administration shunned diplomatic methods of resolving the civil war as recommended by Nathaniel Davis and the State Department Bureau of African Affairs. The US then also abandoned neutrality and acted without the consent of an Angolan government--indeed the intervention was prompted by requests from Zambia and Zaire.

Both the US and the USSR claimed as a rule of the game that intervention required the consent of the government concerned. But they disagreed on the identity of that government, and both acted inconsistently with declared policy in order to support their local clients.

This policy continued with the Ethiopian and Zaire interventions. In both cases the fact that the government requested substantial outside aid constituted grounds for questioning the legitimacy of both the Mengistu and Mobutu regimes. Brownlie (1963:317) has noted that in such situations jurists disagree as to whether the doctrine of consent is sufficient. But such questions were not raised and unlike Angola there were no controversies between the US and the USSR as to the legitimacy of each other's client. This indicated that despite grounds for doing so, each appreciated the mutual benefits of such a practice and that both accepted the rule of consent.

The African reaction to the Shaba II intervention supported this doctrine of consent. At the OAU Khartoum summit of July 18 to 22, 1978, no criticism was raised to the Soviet-Cuban aid to Ethiopia, as long as this did not overstay its welcome. The earlier condemnation of the proposed pan-African force suggested by France (CM/Res. 635/(XXXI)-App. 10) noted that states may take any measure for their security, implying the right to consent to foreign military intervention which was indicated expressly by the Tanzanian representative to the UN to the Secretary-General (Manin 1978:180-183). The resolution on military intervention (CM/Res. 641/(XXXI)-App. 11) reflected the appeal of Obasanjo, the Nigerian President, not to invite in non-African forces but did not repudiate the right to do so, which all African states have claimed as a last resort (Cervenka and Legum 1980:37).

The Soviet intervention in Afghanistan was justified in part as being requested by the Karmal government (_Pravda_ Dec. 29, 1979). Thus the argument raised in the Security Council debate that Amin would not have invited his own executioners into the country is irrelevant. But although professing to follow the rule, the Soviet intervention violated it.

The Soviet intervention in terms of the removal of the Amin government began no later than December 25-26, when 4,000-5,000 troops were airlifted into Kabul. Amin was still head of state at the time. Karmal's request was broadcast from within the USSR; Karmal had been exiled to Eastern Europe following the Khalqi purge of his Parcham faction eighteen months previously. Karmal cannot then legally have invited in the Soviets.

The intervention was intended to depose Amin. He had ousted Taraki in a coup in September, which was an attempt by Taraki to eliminate Amin with Soviet consent, but which backfired. The exact details of the December coup are not certain, but _The Observer_ (Feb. 17, 1980) cited "informed Russian sources in Moscow" to the effect that the coup did not proceed as planned. The intention was to hold elections which Karmal would win and to retain Amin in a lower position in the government. Prior to the intervention Amin was moved for his own safety to the Darulaman Palace, guarded by Afghan soldiers and Soviet military advisers under Lt.-General Victor Paputin, the Soviet First Deputy Minister of Internal Affairs. On December 27 following the arrival of Soviet troops, fighting broke out at the palace and Amin was killed, but not at Soviet hands. There was then an embarrassing vacuum in government for the USSR to cover up hurriedly and unconvincingly. Paputin was recalled to Moscow and committed suicide upon his arrival due to this mistake. However the details may have been, this does not change the fact that the Soviet Union intervened so as to change the government of Afghanistan, making mockery of the rule of consent. Such was the verdict of the United Nations in its resolution condemning the intervention (A/Res. ES-6/2, App. 6).

23

The United States and the Soviet Union have agreed that the consent of governments is required to legitimize interventions. However their practice sheds doubt on the ardour with which they uphold this rule. It was violated in Angola and Afghanistan. In Zaire and Ethiopia it was respected although the need for these interventions constituted grounds for doubting the legitimacy of the governments concerned. On the basis of Soviet and American legal doctrine and practice, this norm counts as a rule of the game, but one frequently breached.

Defense against Aggression:

Similarly the US and the USSR have claimed consistently that military intervention is only permissible if it counters aggression against the target state. But practice has largely violated this rule, indicating the tendency noted by Modelski for an intervener to emphasize the external aspects of a conflict otherwise internal to one state (1961:22).

The justification also raises a further problem in the law of intervention. Collective self-defense is legitimised in Article 51 of the UN Charter (App. 1) but as jurists such as Stassen (1977:76) have pointed out this only covers "armed attack" which is but one type of aggression as in the UN 1974 definition (A/Res. 3314/(XXIX)-App. 3). Yet the Soviet Union and the United States have claimed at least a similar right to intervene to counter other types of aggression, and in the case of Afghanistan explicitly this right under Article 51, creating another gap between doctrine and practice. But under even this broader norm legitimising intervention, practice was largely inconsistent with doctrine.

In Angola, both the Soviet Union and the United States claimed to be abiding by this rule. The

Soviet press highlighted Chinese, American, Zairean and mercenary support to the FNLA and subsequently the South African intervention in October. Reversing earlier descriptions of the conflict as one of civil war (Pravda Aug. 19, 1975), by November 8 Pravda declared that "It is no secret now, that under the guise of a 'civil war', intervention by imperialist and neocolonialist forces has begun in Angola".

The US argued that it was countering by political and financial means the Soviet-Cuban intervention. William Schaufele, Assistant Secretary for African Affairs, explained that the January 1975 decision by the Forty Committee to support Roberto followed the Soviet resumption of arms to the MPLA via Dar-es-Salaam in October 1974. The July decision to intervene militarily followed greater Soviet shipments in the spring (Senate 1976a:175). The Administration denied any collusion with the direct South African intervention (House 1976:156). Following the Security Council condemnation of South Africa on which the US abstained, Kissinger noted that "a more balanced resolution" would have called for the withdrawal of all foreign troops, not just the South Africans (Senate 1976a:11).

The Soviet claim only to be counter-intervening is not tenable. First, their denial of the conflict being internal was inconsistent with their earlier statements and incorrect: the power struggle within Angola drew in foreign intervention. As argued above, the Security Council post facto acceptance of the Soviet position depended largely on African diplomatic opposition to South Africa: recognising the MPLA as the Angola government, the external aspects of the conflict were emphasized to the exclusion of the internal ones. Second, Soviet arms supplies were both substantial and early, being resumed in October 1974 in response to Chinese supplies of arms and trainers to the FNLA in June and July. This preceded American involvement: the Chinese withdrew from the struggle in November 1975.

Third, although the bulk of Cuban troops arrived after the South African intervention of October, some 1,500 of them had reached Luanda by September. So although some case can be made for the Soviet claim given this cycle of involvement, the Soviet-Cuban intervention cannot be characterised as only a counter-move.

The American argument to be reacting to Soviet moves is probably true: indeed the Administration reacted slowly. However it did not follow Davis' advice not to intervene, disregarding his warning that to arm the factions would fuel the civil war (1978). The resulting arms race illustrated the problems of a norm legitimising counter-intervention: resolution of the conflict is not rendered more likely.

In the Ogaden, both sides agreed that this was a case of armed attack by Somalia against Ethiopia, thus justifying the Soviet-Cuban intervention in November 1977. The Soviet press only condemned Somalia openly following the break with Siad Barre (Pravda Nov. 16, 1977) but consistently voiced support for the principle of territorial integrity and non-interference cherished by the OAU (Pravda Aug. 7, 1977) (App. 7). Similarly, the Carter Administration in September withdrew the offer to deliver arms to Somalia as had originally been considered in July once Somali military involvement in the Ogaden became clear (DSB 1977:845). In negotiations with the Somalis on March 19-23, 1978, State Department officials refused to provide arms unless Somalia dropped its claims to the Ogaden and north-eastern Kenya. In May 1978 Vance stated that Barre would have to assure the Administration that he would respect the border and not give "active support" to the West Somali Libera-tion Front (WSLF) fighting in the Ogaden (Senate 1978:5).

The US accepted the Soviet argument to be countering Somali aggression. Vance implicitly conceded this in April 1978 when noting that the withdrawal of Somali forces from the Ogaden removed

26

the "legitimate rationale for the maintenance of
external combat forces" in Ethiopia. Characterizing
the Eritrean conflict as internal, he denied that
Soviet-Cuban intervention there was justified (DSB
1978 (June):25). The Ogaden intervention was the
only case of practice being consistent with the rule
and of both the US and the USSR agreeing on the character of the conflict.

American reaction to unrest in Zaire in 1977
and 1978 was inconsistent. In the former case, Carter
argued that there was no need for direct American
intervention as there was no evidence that the Cubans
were actually in Zaire although they had trained and
armed the FLNC. But in the latter, US involvement was
justified: Brzezinski held that Cuba and "in some
measure" the Soviet Union were "responsible" for Shaba
II but did not hold them guilty of "direct involvement" (DSB 1978 (July):26). Secretary of Defense
Brown admitted that there was no evidence of Cuban
troops having crossed into Shaba (New York Times June
4, 1978). So the American charge amounted to the same
thing in both cases: the Cubans had trained and
armed the ex-Katangan gendarmes but had not intervened
directly. It must be wondered how important this
consideration was given the inconsistency in American
reaction.

The US accusation was substantially correct.
The FLNC was armed with Soviet weapons probably
provided by the Cubans and at least with the acquies-
cence of Angola. The gendarmes had been trained by
Cubans during the Angolan civil war, albeit the FLNC
performance in Shaba did not suggest that it was a
well-trained force.

But these facts arguably did not legitimize
the US intervention. The incursion into Shaba did not
constitute aggression under Article 3(g) of the 1974
definition (App. 3). There is no evidence that the
FLNC was sent "by or on behalf of" Angola, Cuba or
the Soviet Union, and as Mangold has noted even less

27

that East Germany was involved (1979:109). Indeed the Luanda government had clashed with the FLNC over control of the Diaming mine, had attempted to remove Zairean refugees including the Katangans from the border between Shaba I and II, and had difficulty in disarming the FLNC following the latter incident. This suggests that at worst the Angolans and by implication the Cubans were guilty of not controlling the Katangans. Tass statements denying Soviet involvement in both cases were true (Pravda April 13, 1977, May 18, 1978).

Furthermore Zaire at this time had continued to support the FNLA. Both Zaire and Angola had breached their 1976 Brazzaville agreement and their commitments under the OAU resolution on interference in internal affairs of July 5, 1977 (AHG/Res. 85/ (XIV)-App. 9) by not cutting off support for and controlling each other's armed opposition groups. Thus both states bore some responsibility for this state of affairs. This was recognised by Vance when in June 1978 he emphasized that an accord to normalize relations was essential (DSB 1978 (Aug.):12). The US involvement in the Shaba II intervention did not conform to the rule.

The Soviet Union defended its intervention in Afghanistan on the basis of Article 4 of the Soviet-Afghan Treaty of 1978 (App. 12) which provided for "appropriate measures with a view to ensuring the security, independence and territorial integrity of the two countries", and Article 51 of the UN Charter (App. 1) (Pravda Dec. 31, 1979). Carter in his address of January 4, 1980 charged the Soviet Union with aggression and Donald McHenry argued in the Security Council debate that the Soviet intervention violated the Soviet-Afghan Treaty and the UN Charter and was a "perversion" of Article 51 (DSB 1980 (Jan.): A-C).

The General Assembly accepted the American contentions and in Resolution ES-6/2 of January 14

(App. 6) stated that it "strongly deplores the recent
armed intervention in Afghanistan..." and called for
the "withdrawal of the foreign troops" there without
naming their nationality. Having vetoed the Security
Council draft resolution, the Soviet Union condemned
the Assembly one as "obvious interference" in
Afghanistan's internal affairs (Pravda Jan. 16, 1980).
The Islamic Conference resolution of January 28 on the
Soviet intervention was criticised as well (Pravda
Feb. 2, 1980).

The Soviet legal arguments were weak. The
New York Times reported US support to the Afghan
resistance before the intervention (Feb. 17, May 31,
July 21, 1980) which might constitute aggression under
Article 3(g) of the 1974 definition, but which appears
to have been a small financial amount and which was
denied subsequently by the Carter Administration (Feb.
17, 1980). In any event there had not occurred nor
was imminent an "armed attack" such as to justify
invoking Article 51, and its provisions were not
respected. As Meissner has pointed out, the Soviet-
Afghan treaty was not an alliance treaty as those
with the Warsaw Pact members and with Vietnam and did
not provide an automatic right of intervention as
under "socialist internationalist" provisions that
have been incorporated into the WTO treaties since
1970. This would have been required given the
evident lack of a legal invitation (1980:275-280).
Without this, the intervention was both in breach of
the treaty and of the Charter, and constituted aggression under Article 3(a) and (e) of the 1974 definition.

Combined with a request to intervene from the
government, aggression against the target state has
in theory been required to legitimize Soviet and
American military interventions. But this norm has
been breached in three of the four cases. This
suggests that such legal rules of the game were not
considered so important as to be inviolable, but were
sufficiently important that each side felt obliged to
declare adherence to them.

29

Decolonization and Protection of Nationals:

Two other types of legal arguments were employed by the interveners in the cases considered. The USSR appealed to principles of decolonization in Angola and the US argued that the Shaba II intervention was a humanitarian one.

The Soviet claim indicates the vagueness of concepts such as "colonialism" which as Thiele (1978) has pointed out have transformed the norm of non-intervention in the post-colonial world. The Soviet Union, in claiming to have supported the Angolan liberation struggle consistently, slipped from one sense of "colonialism" to another. The first concerned Portuguese rule, the second concerned the South African intervention which showed that "the anticolonial revolution does not end with the achievement of independent statehood" (_Izvestia_ Dec. 26, 1975). Kharlamov, the Soviet Ambassador to the UN, argued that South Africa had intended to reimpose colonial rule on Angola (UN 1976:10).

The Soviet Union has accepted that wars of national liberation are legitimate and that third parties may support these militarily and indeed have a duty to do so (Toman 1975). The United States, on the contrary, while supporting the principle of self-determination has explicitly denied that the decolonization struggle legitimizes intervention by third parties. The US abstained on the vote for the UN General Assembly Resolution on the Implementation of the Declaration on the Granting of Independence to Colonial Countries and Peoples (App. 4), which the Soviet press during the Angolan conflict in 1975 cited in support of its intervention. In agreeing to the Definition of Aggression (A/Res. 3314/(XXIX)-App. 3) in April 1974 Robert Rosenstock, Legal Affairs Adviser to the US Mission to the UN, noted in relation to Article 7 concerning "support" to decolonization that (US Dept. of State 1975:695):

In particular, the Article does not speak of the use of force, but of actions conducted in accordance with the principles of the Charter and the Declaration of Friendly Relations: therefore it is clear that the Article in no way legitimizes acts of armed force by a state which would otherwise constitute aggression.

The legitimacy of military intervention to support wars of national liberation has not then been accepted as a rule of the game by the US.

The Soviet claim to have followed this norm is weak. First, as already remarked it involved a shift in meaning from the struggle against the Portuguese to the conflict with South Africa. In the latter case, there is no evidence that South Africa intended to re-impose colonial rule on Angola as alleged by the USSR. Second, Soviet support to the MPLA was not entirely consistent: in 1973-74 it was switched to Neto's rival Chipenda. Third, the level of Soviet support to the MPLA in 1974-76 was four times the value of that given in the entire period of guerilla war with the Portuguese, indicating a far greater concern for securing a local client's power given the opportunity of a power vacuum than with decolonization. This also applied in the Horn: when backing the Derg, the USSR abandoned its previous support for the Eritrean fight for self-determination. So Soviet practice was not obviously consistent with this norm, which did not in any event qualify as a rule of the game.

Humanitarian intervention and intervention to protect nationals are two controversial rights claimed by states. Brownlie (1963:342) has argued that the former right no longer obtains in international law. Akehurst (1977:16) and Bennouna (1974:174-181) have argued that the latter does not. The United States and other Western countries which have intervened in the Congo since its independence have claimed these as rights, indicating another point of difference

31

between such states and legal scholars. The Soviet
Union criticized the humanitarian aspect of the
intervention as being but a pretext. But it did not
explicitly deny the right in general; rather it
argued that the situation in Shaba did not warrant
intervention and that only other motives were involved
(Izvestia May 24, 1978).

Herbert Hansell, legal advisor to the State
Department, termed the Shaba II intervention "a very
limited, unarmed, humanitarian rescue operation" to
protect Americans, French and Belgians in Kolwezi
threatened by the May 1978 attack (House 1978b:16).
It is not clear whether the intervention was required
for this purpose. All Americans in the area had been
evacuated by their firm. Mbumba, the FLNC leader, was
willing to arrange for the evacuation of the remaining
2,000 Europeans, mostly Belgian, in Kolwezi. An FLNC
envoy had begun to prepare this through the International Red Cross and Belgium was unwilling to attack
Kolwezi, unlike France, so as to allow this to
proceed. However discipline appears to have broken
down among the FLNC, for two hundred Europeans were
reported killed or missing at the time of the intervention. This did not occur in Shaba I, thus
providing some ground for the justification which was
only employed in Shaba II.

Other motives were involved. The US involvement was important as a show of resolve to Mobutu and
by implication to other friendly regimes following the
Soviet-Cuban intervention in Ethiopia. Belgium wished
to limit the intervention to the rescue of Europeans
from Kolwezi; France on the other hand also employed
its legionaires to push the FLNC back and indicated
that it wished to expand its security role in Zaire.
The practice of either humanitarian intervention or
of rescue of nationals has always involved mixed
motives and it is moot whether the doctrine permits
this or not. As Manin has noted, the legality in
recent practice appears to rest on the doctrine of
consent (1978:164-170). Thus as a rule of the game

it is at best conditional upon that, and the nature of the rule itself is open to some controversy on the question of mixed motives.

Neither of these candidates for rules of the game appears to be very promising. Both were used infrequently, with some question as to the consistency with doctrine, and neither was accepted unambiguously by both the US and the USSR in these cases.

Conclusion:

Two legal rules of the game emerge from consideration of these four cases. Military intervention must have the consent of the government of the target state. It must also be aimed at countering aggression against that state. But although the US and the USSR agreed on these rules, their practice was not always consistent with them. They frequently disagreed on the nature of the conflict and of the actors involved: they defined "the government" and "the aggressors" to suit their own interests. Both were willing to ignore qualms about the rules and the legitimacy of governments in order to back Third World regimes and in many cases were prepared to infringe these rules to this end. The rules were considered sufficiently important to be used to justify military intervention, but not so important that they were not violated or mis-applied.

33

3. SOVIET-AMERICAN DETENTE

The 1970s were understood to be a period of
Soviet-American detente, which to a large extent was
alleged in the US to be wrecked by Soviet military
interventions in the Third World. The US argued that
these infringed the "code of detente". To the extent
that a specific agreement was indicated by this, it
was the Basic Principles of Relations between the US
and the USSR (App. 13), a non-legal yet binding
accord, signed by Nixon and Brezhnev in May 1972. On
the other side, the Soviet Union argued that its
military interventions did not infringe the detente
agreement, and that any American counter-moves such
as economic sanctions or military action did infringe
it. In order to settle the argument, it must be
determined whether detente established any rules of
the game.

The Basic Principles would be the most
obvious starting-point. But the two states clearly
interpreted these differently, at least as far as
military intervention in the Third World was concerned. What criteria are there for a correct interpretation? Here the lack of any secondary rule to
deal with this, besides the consent of the states
concerned, does not help. It is not clear that there
is any obviously correct interpretation, such that
either party's disagreement with it can be dismissed
as totally implausible. As Kissinger conceded, "I
did not believe that history would remember a set of
principles so watered down as to be equally acceptable

to the principal capitalist and the strongest Communist state" (1979:1150). So the only available criterion is one of mutual understanding of the spirit of the detente agreement.

However such mutual understanding was totally lacking, as the following discussion will show. There is then no basis for speaking of the rules of detente --in the sense of rules agreed upon by both states-- and therefore no basis for claiming that either state did or did not break these rules in intervening militarily in the Third World. Furthermore, the Soviet and American practice during the period of detente until the Soviet intervention in Afghanistan suggested that on the basis of tacit consent, the two powers did not link their rivalry in the Third World with other areas of their relationship. Although they did not accept each other's interventions to be legitimate, they did consent to them in the sense of not opposing them militarily, again until Afghanistan. Under the constraints of relative power considerations, military intervention was accepted as part of that rivalry in the Third World.

American Detente - The Balance of Power:

The American understanding of detente was bound up with what the Nixon Administration considered to be a reappraisal of American foreign policy in the early 1970s. It emphasized multipolarity, the recognition of US global over-extension, and the need for negotiation with the communist states. However it was also committed to the doctrine of maintaining the global balance of power, and this strongly influenced the American understanding of detente and so their interpretation of its rules for Third World military intervention.

The Nixon Administration spoke of a framework of "peace" in its first annual report on foreign policy to the Congress (President 1970:5-8). This was comprised of three elements. "Partnership" required a shift to multilateral rather than unilateral commitments. "Strength" required the maintenance of "an irreducible minimum of essential military security" while recognizing the approach to strategic parity by the Soviet Union. Thirdly, the US must be willing to negotiate with the communist states despite "enduring ideological differences".

The theme of "partnership" stressed a recognition of the multipolar nature of global power. This applied to both the West and its allies and to the communist bloc. As regards the former, the US could legitimately redistribute its security burden to its partners. This was also required as a response to American over-extension, especially in Vietnam, in direct military intervention and in the organization of the local infrastructure, which taxed America's "psychological resources" and so elicited domestic opposition to such extreme commitments. The Nixon Doctrine responded to this by curtailing direct American military intervention and reviewing overseas commitments. But it was not a retreat into isolationism. Rather it involved keeping treaty commitments so as to maintain stability and credibility among client regimes, providing a nuclear shield to allies threatened by the communist powers, and by assisting with military and economic means allies threatened by aggression (President 1971:9).

The Nixon Doctrine involved a balance of power philosophy marked by four features. First, it tended to adopt a global perspective to problems, such as political change in the Third World, and viewed this in terms of competition with the Soviet Union--as the adversary communist power--rather than in terms of local conditions. The multipolar world thesis modified this somewhat, but not in the face of Soviet military influence. Even US policy under Andrew Young in the Carter Administration stressed the use of non-military means to combat the expansion of Soviet

influence. Second, it was marked by fear of instability in client regimes and assumed that this favoured
the USSR. Third, it emphasized the need to maintain
credibility with local allies in the face of Soviet
military activity. Fourth, a range of means to maintain these commitments were contemplated, including
indirect intervention, but with direct intervention
after Vietnam as an unlikely last recourse. Indeed
the greatest modification in US practice in this
period was in this area: in both Vietnam and Angola
in 1975, the Ford Administration was unable to secure
Congressional approval for its planned indirect interventions. The Carter Administration considered the
transfer of arms to be the furthest extent to which it
would intervene in local conflicts, until the Soviet
intervention in Afghanistan.

This failure to play the balance of power game
fully could not be blamed on detente. When asked
whether Soviet aid to North Vietnam violated detente,
Kissinger replied (DSB 1975a:668):

What we cannot ask the Soviet Union to do is
to keep itself from taking advantages of
situations in which, for whatever reason, we
do not do what is required to maintain the
balance....

Maintaining the balance was presupposed as an integral
part of detente. In Kissinger's view it was "based on
the element of resistance to expansion" (Senate 1976b:
499). Due to its size and location, the USSR was
considered to have legitimate security interests in
Eastern Europe and East Asia, but to try and gain
"predominant positions" elsewhere was not considered
legitimate (President 1971:55). Kissinger explained
that (DSB 1973:528):

Coexistence, to us, continues to have a very
precise meaning:
- We will oppose the attempt by any country
to achieve a position of predominance either
globally or regionally.

38

        - We will resist any attempt to exploit a
policy of detente to weaken our alliances.
        - We will react if relaxation of tensions
is used as a cover to exacerbate local
conflicts in international trouble spots.

The "unilateral gain" provision of the second principle of the May 1972 accord was interpreted by the US
as prohibiting Soviet advances beyond their sphere of
influence, whether this be subversion in Portugal or
direct intervention in Africa. The US interpreted
detente to be an agreement on preserving the existing
balance of power both globally and regionally.

        The US assumed that this consideration would
apply to both sides (President 1972:12):

        A broad and mutual self-restraint was essential.
        If either side sought to gain significant
        advantage over the other, it would inevitably
        lead to counter-actions aimed at redressing the
        balance. That in turn would jeopardize any
        progress that had already been achieved, and
        make infinitely more difficult the task of
        reaching agreements on the specific issues
        which divide us.

So the American conception of detente presupposed the
linkage of separate issues as well as maintenance of
the balance of power. Negotiations with the Soviet
Union must address the need to deal with a broad range
of issues because they were interrelated, and link
these so as to create "a broadly based understanding
about international conduct" (President 1973:14).

        The pursuit of detente rested on the assess-
ment that it was in the interests of neither the US
nor the communist states to continue their relations
on a conflictual basis. The President's report noted
that (President 1970:49):

        At issue are basic questions of long conflict-
        ing purposes in a world where no one's interests

are furthered by conflict. Only a straight
forward recognition of that reality--and an
equally direct effort to deal with it--will
bring us to the genuine cooperation which
we seek, and which the peace of the world
requires.

There were two considerations which overrode interest
in the maintenance of tension, and which applied
equally to both sides in the Administration's view.
First, the danger of nuclear war and the need to
maintain the balance of power would push both sides
to seek solutions to their differences via negotiations. Second, local conflicts in which the great
powers were deeply involved raised the problem of
possible confrontations in situations in which there
was little control of local forces, and this too
created a need for peacefully regulating such conflict.

These assessments involved assumptions about
the Soviet view of conflict. The report stated that
(President 1970:47):

The Communist world in particular has had to
learn that the spread of Communism may
magnify international tensions rather than
usher in a period of reconciliation as Marx
taught.

As will be discussed below, this did not accurately
portray the Soviet attitude to conflict in the Third
World. The failure of the Nixon Administration to
appreciate this stemmed at least in part from its
conviction that "it was no longer realistic to allow
Soviet-American relations to be predetermined by
ideology"; although the values of the two states
would remain inimical, this "did not preclude serious
consideration of disputed interests" (President 1973:
14). This suggested a separation between "ideology"
and "interests" which it is argued below is untenable
in Soviet foreign policy. It therefore led the

40

Administration to discount Soviet pronouncements
which indicated that the Soviet leadership saw the
continuance of East-West conflict in the Third World
as compatible with negotiation and reduced tension in
other areas. The American view was that competition
would remain but that (President 1973:14):

> There would be no permanent victor, and,
> ... that to focus one's own policy on
> attempts to gain advantages at the other's
> expense could only aggravate tensions and
> precipitate counteractions.

The Soviets disagreed with the first proposition, and
saw nothing amiss with the second.

The Nixon Administration and its successors
did not entirely ignore the continuing competitive
aspects of Soviet-American relations. Kissinger
remarked that "the very concept of 'detente' has
always been applicable only to an adversary relationship" (Kissinger 1976:198). It had two dimensions:
the resolution of conflict through negotiations and
the prevention of Soviet military strength furthering
political expansion. The rivalry would continue but
"detente encourages an environment in which competi-
tors can regulate and restrain their differences and
ultimately move from competition to co-operation"
(Kissinger 1975:35). Brzezinski emphasized that the
competitive aspects were still "predominant" and that
detente has never been "the equivalent of a compre-
hensive, indeed total accommodation between the United
States and the Soviet Union" (DSB 1978 (July):27).
This attitude not surprisingly grew as Soviet interventions in the Third World gradually impressed the
Soviet understanding of detente on the Ford and Carter
Administrations.

However the understanding was slow to develop.
Before the 1972 Moscow summit, the Nixon Administra-
tion was concerned that the Soviet arms build-up and
Soviet actions in the Middle East and during the
Indian-Pakistani war made it:

unclear whether we are now witnessing a
permanent change in Soviet policy or only
a passing phase concerned more with tactics
than with a fundamental commitment to a
stable international system (President
1972:8).

However, rather as the Soviet leadership decided not
to cancel the meeting due to the American mining of
Haiphong, so the US concluded that progress on other
fronts made a summit appropriate. Fears that the
Soviets might not share the American conception of "a
stable international system" were not seriously enter-
tained (President 1972:12):

The expansion of Soviet military and economic
resources has made feasible a steady expansion of the Soviet presence in the Middle
East, in South Asia, and in other areas. As
it increases its influence, however, the
Soviet Union also acquires responsibilities,
and hopefully a new interest in regional
stability. To the degree the USSR exercises
its influence in the interests of restraint,
the USSR and the US could act on parallel
courses.

This hopefullness was to be ill-founded, and the
Soviet interventions in Angola, Ethiopia and Afghanistan changed this expectation that the USSR would
become a status quo power.

The American understanding of detente was
marked by four key features. First, it required that
the Soviet Union and the United States should maintain
global and regional balances of power. Second, it
required linking of issues such as instability in the
Third World with other superpower relations so as to
enhance preservation of the balance by non-military
means. Third, it assumed that the Soviet Union had
the same view as did the United States concerning the
value of conflict and the maintenance of tension in
the Third World. Fourth, it also assumed that the

42

Soviet Union would see its relations with the US as a web of mutual interests rather than as separate issues. Both assumptions were incorrect, and neither requirement was fulfilled. The error of the assumptions meant that American pronouncements concerning the "spirit of detente" were just American viewpoints: there was no mutual agreement on this. The failure of the requirements to be met signified the failure of American detente policy as it had been conceived.

Soviet Detente - The Correlation of Forces:

The Soviet understanding of detente was entirely different from the American. First, rather than representing an agreement to preserve the status quo in the Third World by maintaining the balance of power, the Soviet Union interpreted detente as legitimizing changes in that balance. Second, rather than involving a web of mutual interests on all levels of superpower relations, the Soviets argued that developments in the Third World were separate from Soviet-American relations on other issues such as bilateral trade, strategic arms negotiations, and multilateral affairs in Europe. Third, the Soviets held the first view because they saw detente as arising out of a favourable shift in the correlation of forces, which stressed the continuation and intensification of the class struggle in the newly-liberated nations. Fourth, the Soviet rejection of the concept of linkage reflected their view that relations between states depended on their class basis, and that therefore detente did not apply to the relations of either the Soviet Union or the United States with the Third World. The US regarded detente as prohibiting military intervention in that region unless it was in defense of the status quo. The Soviet Union, in rejecting the legitimacy of that status quo, held that such action ran contrary to detente but that intervention in support of the progressive forces was permitted.

In order to comprehend the Soviet perspective on these points, Soviet doctrine concerning relations between states and class forces requires explanation. To dismiss such an approach as revealing only ideological statements and missing the key features of Soviet thinking about power and interests is incorrect. As Kubalkova and Cruikshank (1981) as well as other authors have argued, Soviet ideology is explicitly about power and provides evidence for the attitudes and intentions of the leadership. Soviet interests are defined and explained in terms which are ideological such that the two are not logically separable.

Soviet understanding of events such as these interventions involves a global perspective, with the socialist system and the progressive forces on the one hand and on the other their protagonist, the capitalist system led by the United States and aided by its accomplice China. Such a view involves both state- and class-based aspects.

At the state level, Moscow sees itself as the centre of the world socialist system, which radiates onion-like around it. The USSR is its leader as the first socialist state. Next comes the socialist bloc of East European countries, Cuba, Vietnam and Mongolia. In the Third World stand various newly-liberated states of socialist orientation, including Angola, Ethiopia and Afghanistan.

At the class level, there exists an over-lapping grouping of progressive forces. Again, the Soviet Union led by the CPSU constitutes its centre, followed by the ruling communist parties in the socialist bloc. In the capitalist world lie the non-ruling working-class parties. On the periphery are the forces of national liberation in Asia, Africa and South America.

The ambiguity possible with such overlapping concepts is immediately apparent. The same actors assume different roles either on the state level or on the class level and so their actions are open to varying interpretations. This constitutes a source of confusion and dispute, particularly given the detente relationship.

The imperialist camp includes North America, Western Europe and Japan and is led by the United States. As Roberts (1977) has explained, "imperialism" in current Soviet usage simply refers to these countries and is equivalent to "advanced monopoly capitalism"--the crucial feature of the export of surplus capital from Lenin's theory, coupled with the possession of colonies, has been dropped. Imperialism constitutes the greatest threat to socialism, particularly in the guise of NATO. The two systems are locked in inevitable conflict, although this march of history can be coloured with periods of relaxed tensions, increased trade and negotiations on strategic arms limitations. China is seen as supporting the imperialist camp: although Soviet spokesmen have not denied that she is socialist, relations with China are categorised under peaceful coexistence, which as Kubalkova and Cruikshank have pointed out is inconsistent with the doctrine that state-to-state relations depend on the class basis of each state (1978:195).

Recent theoretical writing indicates a trend back towards conceiving global political power in bipolar terms. Kim, expressing recent Soviet views, has written that "the 1970s refuted the imperialist and Maoist assertions that there is a united 'third world' following a previously unknown 'third road' to social progress" (1980:70). Rather "the differentiation of the newly-free states of Asia and Africa by socio-economic and political structures was completed" (63). This division into states of socialist- and capitalist-orientation represents the Soviet view that in these areas political alignments are becoming more polarized, as these in theory are dependent on social development, albeit in practice the level of social development ascribed to different states in Soviet writing depends on their political alignment. Western and Chinese theories "about the 'exclusiveness' of the non-aligned movement, its 'equidistance' from the two world systems" are dismissed (Sovetskaya Rossiya April 18, 1980). Although its "natural ally" is the socialist bloc (Pravda Aug. 12, 1976), alignment is seen in terms of either-or with no middle ground or third world.

The socialist and capitalist blocs are seen to be engaged in inevitable conflict. The correlation of forces is an intuitive calculation of the balance between the two camps. It is based on economic and military strength, political stability and flexibility, and the cohesion and motivation of international movements (Deane 1976). It is conceived in dynamic terms. The correlation is seen to have shifted dramatically on three occasions: at the establishment of the Soviet state in 1917, on the formation of the socialist system after 1945, and at the achievement by the USSR of strategic nuclear parity with the US in 1969-1970. By contrast, talk of the balance of power is rejected as the Soviet Union does not accept the implied legitimacy of the status quo (Wessell 1979).

The class-state ambiguity is evident in employment of this concept. It is used to mark indigenous social and political change in favour of the progressive forces. But it also refers to the improved military balance between the USSR and the US, which was the last decisive shift in the correlation and of which the Nixon Administration was also aware.

The Soviet Union considers detente to have resulted from this shift: as such, detente represents a concession of weakness by the United States. This was formalized in the recognition of Soviet strategic parity by the US in SALT I and also in the Basic

Principles' "recognition of the security interests of the parties based on the principle of equality". In reviewing the 1970s, Nekrasov in Kommunist linked detente explicitly with this change in the military balance (1980:27):

> The main reason for the successes achieved by the policy of detente in the preceding period was that it derived legitimately from the increased international role of the socialist countries and the influence of their coordinated policy on the world situation. The June 1980 CC CPSU Plenum described the military-strategic balance achieved between the socialist and the capitalist worlds as a gain of essential and historic significance.... [The policy of detente] also reflected the more realistic approach adopted by a number of Western political leaders in their assessment of the global situation.

The results of detente were particularly marked in the newly-liberated countries such as Angola, Ethiopia and Afghanistan. Ponomarev (1980:33) remarked on the:

> Major success achieved by the policy of detente, as a result of which the so-called 'maneuvering freedom' of most aggressive imperialist forces was substantially restricted....

Detente to the Soviet Union involved an explicit rejection of Nixon-Kissinger balance of power thinking. Soviet commentary has emphasized a bipolar view of international affairs. The conception of a pentagonal balance of power was held "to impede the strengthening of the position of socialism and the growth of revolutionary and national liberation movements" (Karenin 1975:102). But this shift in the correlation of forces is precisely what detente legitimized to the Soviet leadership, and the American leadership was held to have acquiesced to this.

The favourable changes in the correlation of forces are depicted as part of the objective laws of history which are held to be immutable. In this context Soviet leaders emphasize the indigenous roots of revolutionary change in the Third World. Arbatov noted that the victory of the MPLA in Angola could not "seriously" be ascribed solely to the support it received from the Soviet Union and Cuba (Pravda April 2, 1976). Similarly Zamyatin argued (Literaturnya gazeta Feb. 27, 1980):

> But it is by no means through the Soviet Union's efforts that decayed regimes collapse or the independence of one country or another is established. Changes such as these in Iran and Afghanistan, for example, come to fruition only on national soil. To ascribe them, as the US administration does, to 'Moscow's machinations' is to delude oneself and the public.

This follows the Leninist tradition of using an already developed revolution in order to intervene, as the Bolsheviks did in their 1917 coup.

The Soviet military role is not denied. Soviet leaders are proud of their contributions to the revolutionary process in the Third World. In this way use of the changed correlation of forces is very much a matter of policy. This was foreshadowed in a change in military doctrine. Marshall Ustinov wrote that under developed socialism the role of the army was no longer an internal one against class enemies but rather was to protect socialist gains from external threats (Pravda Feb. 23, 1973). This military role is clearly implied in Soviet commentary concerning solidarity with the progressive forces (cited in Dahm 1976:108):

> But this support comes not through export of revolution or immixation from outside, but above all through measures aimed at parrying

the counter-revolutionary blows of reac-
tionaries everywhere and at preventing the
interference of the imperialist forces in
the internal affairs of other countries and
peoples.

Such "support" particularly involves the Soviet navy,
which under Admiral Gorshkov has extended its range
of operations to regions such as the Indian Ocean.

Such action comes under the principles of
proletarian internationalism which oblige the world
progressive forces to support each other in their
struggle: these are a species of class-based rather
than state-based principles. As Sanakoyev explained,
"proletarian internationalism reliably safeguards
the revolutionary gains of the peoples and blocks the
export of counter-revolution" beyond the bounds of
the socialist commonwealth (1980:90). Thus it
legitimizes Soviet military intervention in what can
be regarded as new spheres of influence, as will be
argued below. The change in the correlation of forces
allots an expansive role to the Soviet Union in
military affairs, in contrast to the American prefer-
ence for maintenance of the existing balance.

To Soviet commentators such as Sidenko, this
American attitude merely confirmed that the class
struggle continued in the developing countries despite
detente (1980:89):

But while accepting detente [the imperialists]
also pursued their own class aims. It is not
accidental that since the early 1970s Western
ideologists and politicians have been closely
linking the policy of detente with the
struggle against revolutionary and national
liberation movements and viewing detente as
a sort of guarantee against new revolutionary
upheavals in various regions of the capitalist
world.

49

American attempts to counter Soviet moves as after the latter's intervention in Afghanistan indicated to the USSR a departure from detente by the US--a departure from recognition of and consent to the use of Soviet military power to support the progressive forces.

American military intervention in the Third World has always been regarded as illegitimate in Soviet doctrine, being a feature of "neocolonialism". The Soviets did not initially articulate such a view as constituting part of detente. The Moscow summit of 1972 followed shortly after the mining of Haiphong. The Soviets did not cancel the meeting and made what Kissinger regarded as only a ritual denunciation of American intervention in Vietnam (1979:1227). Arbatov (1973) noted that this complicated progress towards detente without explicitly holding that it was inconsistent with it.

However following the formalization of detente the Soviet leadership explicitly held American interventions to be incompatible with it. At the 60th Anniversary of the October Revolution in 1977, Brezhnev noted that the results of detente included:

> ...recognising and enacting in international documents a kind of code of rules for honest and fair relations between countries, which erects a legal and a moral and political barrier in the way of those given to military gambles...

as in the American intervention in Vietnam (1978:33). American actions such as the Shaba II intervention, enunciation of the Carter Doctrine and creation of a Rapid Deployment Force were contrary to detente. As Ponomarev noted in relation to national and social liberation in the developing countries, "the policy of 'antidetente' and neocolonialist revenge are profoundly interlinked" (1980:37).

So the Soviet Union classified relations between both the capitalist bloc and the socialist commonwealth on the one hand and the developing countries on the other in class terms: intervention in the one case being illegitimate neocolonialism and in the other legitimate international proletarian solidarity. What then were the relations between the capitalist and socialist blocs, and in particular how did the Soviets answer the American charge that Soviet interventions violated detente?

Relations between states depend in theory on their class basis. Detente is a species of peaceful coexistence. This consists of the principles of equality, respect for sovereignty, and noninterference in internal affairs and holds only between states of different social systems. The formulation of the Principles is simply an elaboration of this in the Soviet view. Erikson has noted that the Soviet equivalent of detente, razryadka, is a tactical option set within the broader framework of peaceful coexistence (1976:40). Detente therefore also applies only to capitalist and socialist states: it does not apply to relations between either of these and the newly-liberated nations.

Arbatov (1973) noted that under detente Soviet-American relations would be directed away from "military confrontations, the arms race, intense and dangerous conflicts" towards the peaceful "ideological struggle of the two systems ... in which inevitable differences are settled by negotiation...." But as Karen Brutents explained, this did not affect Soviet military support to the progressive forces in the Third World (1979:5):

> Imperialist propaganda maintains that there is a contradiction between the Soviet Union's line for detente, and its relations with the newly-independent countries and its support for national liberation movements. This contradiction, however, is purely imaginary. The point is that detente and peaceful coexistence apply to interstate relations.

51

> Detente does not and cannot change or
> repeal the laws of anti-imperialist
> struggle, while the people's struggle for
> liberation and national statehood and the
> support they receive during it are in full
> agreement with the spirit of peaceful co-
> existence...

which presupposes the eventual victory of the progressive forces. Competition in direct Soviet-American
relations--state-to-state ones--could be restrained
and reach negotiated settlements. But class conflict
was not abolished, but rather channelled into the
Third World. This differed completely from the American conception of detente wherein all of these issues
should be linked in order to prevent just this division.

The Soviet conception of detente and the
correlation of forces contrasts sharply with the
American conception of detente and the balance of
power. First, while the US moved towards conceiving
global power in multipolar terms, the USSR moved
towards seeing it in bipolar terms. Second, the US
saw conflict with the communist bloc as ultimately
resoluble, with at least some possibility of co-
operation; the Soviet Union saw conflict between the
socialist and capitalist blocs as fundamental,
ultimately to result in the victory of the former,
with negotiations on immediate issues nonetheless of
value. Third, the United States considered detente
to rely on maintenance of the global and regional
balances of power and prohibit Soviet unilateral gains
outside of their sphere of influence. The Soviet
Union saw detente as arising from a shift in the
correlation of forces in their favour, amounting to
an admission of weakness by the United States, and
rather than legitimising maintenance of the status quo
in the Third World permitting Soviet interventions to
aid the progressive forces and so in American eyes
change that status quo. Fourth, while the Nixon
Doctrine represented an American retreat from the

previous practice of direct military intervention, the development of the Soviet doctrines of war and of proletarian internationalism represented a greater willingness and capacity to intervene in Third World conflicts. Fifth, the United States considered that all areas of Soviet-American relations should be interwoven to create a system of sanctions and induce- ments. The Soviet Union on the other hand held that state-to-state relations with the capitalist nations were entirely separate from the Soviet role in the class struggle in the newly-liberated countries, and that therefore there would be no incompatibility between that role and its agreements with the US. As far as the Third World was concerned, the two parties approached detente from such radically different perspectives that no agreement on a rule of the game concerning military intervention could be expected.

Angola:

The US protest against Soviet intervention in Angola raised the question of restraints on such action as embodied in the detente relationship. In his speech at Detroit of November 24, 1975, Kissinger stated that "we will never permit detente to turn into a subterfuge for unilateral advantage" noting that this intervention was "difficult to reconcile with" the Principles (DSB 1975:843). Kissinger was referring to the second principle, in which "both sides recognize that efforts to obtain unilateral advantage at the expense of the other, directly or indirectly, are inconsistent with these objectives" of exercising "restraint in their mutual relations" so as "to avoid military confrontations and to prevent the outbreak of nuclear war" (App. 13). Kissinger's position was endorsed by Ford the next day (DSB 1975: 895).

In the Senate hearings on Angola in January 1976, Kissinger noted that although competition with

53

the Soviets would continue under detente, it was to be directed away from military to political and economic means: "if military means became again the accepted standard, then eventually all international restraints will disappear" (Senate 1976a:33). An attempt "to gain a unilateral advantage" by installing a regime by force was unacceptable (52). The Soviet gains of concern were specified by Robert Ellsworth, Deputy Secretary of Defense. They included naval bases, air overflight paths and refuelling stops, a possible threat to Cape ocean traffic, a potential danger to the peaceful resolution of the conflicts in Rhodesia, Namibia and South Africa, and a danger of insurgency to Zaire and Zambia (60-63).

The Soviet Union replied sharply to the Detroit speech, accusing "certain top leaders in the USA" of distorting the picture of the Angolan conflict. "They deliberately present the matter as though the source of the tension in southern Africa were not the racist regime of the Republic of South Africa and its aggression but rather the struggle against racism and aggression" (Izvestia Dec. 26, 1975). At the XXVth CPSU Congress, Brezhnev stressed that the obligation under proletarian internationalism to render aid to the MPLA was not incompatible with detente (Pravda Feb. 25, 1976). Rather, "aggression" and "colonialist plunder ... create tensions and are a threat to the peace" as a Pravda editorial observed (Jan. 3, 1976). Furthermore, "as far as detente is concerned, the struggle against racism and apartheid and the defense of and respect for the sovereignty of young independent nations is indeed also a contribution to detente..." (Izvestia Jan. 7, 1976). The Soviets claimed their intervention to be compatible with and supportive of detente.

The US did not press its claims convincingly. First, the signal which they sent to the Soviets was ambiguous: on the one hand they condemned the intervention; on the other, Kissinger refused to link it with the SALT negotiations (DSB 1976a:125) and Ford ruled out cutting grain shipments in retaliation (New York Times Jan. 6, 1976). The New York Times cited "high US officials" as saying that the Soviet intervention was not linked to detente, but rather that they could not do this in an election year (Dec. 17). The Soviets would then have grounds for holding that events in Angola were not linked to other Soviet-American relations: given the factor of Soviet competition with China in Angola the intervention probably appeared peripheral to Soviet-American relations to Moscow. Second, the United States had itself been involved in Angola, and the Soviets could have interpreted this as an indication that the Ford Administration considered such military competition to be acceptable within the detente framework (Kaplan 1981:198). This is supported by the fact that the first public criticism of Soviet involvement came as late as September 24 in Kissinger's address to African diplomats (New York Times Sept. 25, 1975). The internal debate on the July decision to support the anti-MPLA forces militarily as reported by Davis (1978) did not raise the question of the compatibility of such action with detente. The Administration was curtailed from intervening to the extent that it wished to by domestic opposition, not by detente.

Kissinger argued that maintaining the balance of power regionally as well as globally was an essential part of detente (Senate 1976b:499). Therefore what he judged to be an American counter-intervention was justified within the detente framework. But this would presuppose an agreement on sustaining the balance in an area such as Southern Africa: the Soviets have always explicitly stated that they would not accept such an arrangement. Each side intervened, albeit at different levels, consistent with their own interpretation of detente. However the US failed to link the Soviet intervention with other issues; coupled with the limitations of its intervention, this indicated that the two main strands of American detente policy failed to be applied fully in Angola.

The Horn:

The Carter Administration played on the detente relationship in connection with Soviet intervention in the Horn to a lesser extent than had its predecessor in Angola. Meeting Ponomarev in Washington, Carter warned him that improved relations between the two countries would depend on the USSR reducing its growing military involvement in the Horn (New York Times Jan. 26, 1978). The State Department noted that the "character of general relations depends upon restraint and constructive efforts to help resolve local conflicts, such as the Horn of Africa" (New York Times Feb. 26, 1978). And Carter emphasized that "in the strongest possible terms we have let the Soviets and the Cubans know that this is a danger to American-Soviet friendship and to the nurturing and enhancement of the principle of detente" (DSB 1978 (July):21).

The United States employed a sanction. Vance announced that the Soviet-Cuban intervention was "inconsistent with a limitation of forces" in the Indian Ocean (DSB 1978 (March):15). Leslie Gelb, a State Department aide, later testified before the House Committee on International Affairs that increased Soviet naval activity in the Indian Ocean due to the Ogaden intervention led the US to suspend talks on freezing military operations there (New York Times Oct. 4, 1978).

However the Administration chose not to link the issue with conclusion of SALT II. Brzezinski noted that although Soviet military involvement in the Horn could complicate efforts to achieve this, the US would not formally link progress on this with the situation in Africa (New York Times March 2, 1978). As in Angola, the Administration was reluctant to employ such sanctions involving vital issues. Brzezinski later concluded that (1981:28):

I have said that 'SALT lies buried in the

sands of the Ogaden', because I do feel that
our under-reaction at the time emboldened
the Soviets to be more assertive, thus
creating in time a strong US public reaction
which eventually precluded the ratification
of SALT.

Soviet commentators criticized any suggestion
of linking the SALT talks with "issues that have no
bearing whatsoever on the problems of arms limitations,
in particular, with the situation on the Horn of
Africa..." (Pravda March 5, 1978). Arbatov noted that
such a connection "is totally inappropriate when the
matter in hand is an agreement in which both sides
have an equal interest, not some kind of 'prize' for
the Soviet Union". However he agreed that the events
in the Horn of Africa "will affect the political
situation making agreement on SALT more difficult"
(Pravda March 28, 1978).

Both the Soviet Union and the United States
appreciated that such conflicts could sour relations
generally and make negotiations on other issues,
especially on strategic nuclear arms, more difficult.
Both also opposed linking the situation in the Horn
with SALT. The former was peripheral to the central
relationship embodied in the latter.

Shaba II and Retrospective on the Horn:

Following the events in Shaba in May 1978,
there was a vituperative exchange between American
leaders and authoritative Soviet press statements
concerning detente and events in both Africa and the
Middle East. The Carter Administration faced a
cumulation of worrisome events. Vance discerned a
"pattern" of Soviet involvement in Angola, Ethiopia,
South Yemen and Afghanistan which threatened detente,
which "has to be a two-way street. They [the Soviets]
understand our position on that" (Senate 1978:14).

Brzezinski considered detente to involve competition and co-operation, with principles of restraint on the former. However recent Soviet actions "... to encircle and penetrate the Middle East, to stir up racial difficulties in Africa..." were not compatible with "the code of detente" (DSB 1978 (July):27). Carter depicted the Soviet conception of detente as "a continuing aggressive struggle for political advantage and increased influence" particularly involving the projection of military power into "areas of instability". Inviting the Soviets to choose between confrontation and co-operation, he warned that "a competition without restraint and without shared rules will escalate into graver tensions, and our relationship as a whole with the Soviet Union will suffer" (DBS 1978 (July):15).

The Soviet verbal counter-attack was sharp. Brzezinski's characterisation of detente was noted without challenge, indicating that the Soviet leadership shared it. However he had presented the "USSR's foreign policy in a false light" concerning activities in the Middle East and Africa. It was not the Soviet Union which was aggravating tension in Africa, but the US-organized intervention in Zaire (Pravda May 31, 1978). Gromyko held that the "bourgeois propaganda campaign" about Soviet and Cuban involvement in Ethiopia served in part to cover the Zaire intervention (Pravda June 3, 1978). A Soviet government statement noted that (Pravda June 23, 1978):

> While making hypocritical statements about the 'indivisibility of detente' and the need to extend it to all regions of the globe, the NATO countries, and especially the US, are actually acting in precisely the opposite direction in Africa.

Such "neocolonialist" ventures ran contrary to the Soviet conception of detente.

What also was not compatible with detente were the criticisms voiced by the Carter Administration, the Soviet argument continued. These indicated that "factions" were gaining power "that would like to undermine detente and return the world to the cold war and new confrontations...." It was the US, not the Soviet Union, which had yet to choose between conflict and co-operation (_Pravda_ June 17, 1978). Gromyko reversed the American accusation: it was the American position vis-à-vis Africa which was worsening the atmosphere required to conclude the SALT agreement (_Pravda_ June 3, 1978).

Each side condemned the other's military intervention on the basis of their respective understandings of detente. The Soviets adopted a new line in this series of exchanges, holding the US responsible for the worsening of relations. This is consistent with the Soviet doctrine of taking detente to apply to relations between only capitalist and socialist states and so at least publicly disclaiming that African interventions by it should affect that relationship adversely.

Afghanistan:

The Soviet intervention of December 1979 was the first to be answered with major detente-related sanctions. In his address to the nation of January 4, 1980, Carter announced a review of Soviet-American relations which would include a ban on the sale of high technology, curtailment of fishing privileges, a ban on grain sales in excess of amounts already contracted, and the deferral of the SALT II treaty for Senate ratification (DSB 1980 (Jan.):A-B). Although Carter did not explicitly mention detente, this was the clearest signal to the Soviet Union that the US considered such interventions to be contrary to detente.

The reaction of other members of the Administration was more ambiguous. Warren Christopher,

the Deputy Secretary of State, stated that "I don't
think it is time to pronounce the death of detente...."
Rather it was a question of demonstrating the "cost"
of aggression to the USSR (DSB 1980 (Feb.):6). Vance
held that "nor is it in our interest, during a period
of heightened tensions, to dismantle the framework of
East-West relations that have been built over more
than two decades" referring to SALT and the Conference
on Security and Cooperation in Europe (DSB 1980
(April):13). On the other hand, Marshall Shulman, the
Secretary's Special Adviser on Soviet Affairs,
concluded that detente as known since 1972 "has been
dead a long time" given turbulence in the Third World
and the failure to ratify SALT (House 1980:28). He
admitted the failure "to reach agreement on some
Marquis of Queensbury rules on how to conduct the
competition" (58). The Carter Administration held the
intervention to be incompatible with detente, but it
was less clear whether it considered that relationship
to still obtain or not.

The Soviet Union charged that the sanctions
announced by Carter were contrary to detente (Pravda
Jan. 6, 1980):

> These measures, borrowed from the arsenal of
> the cold war, constitute a flagrant violation
> by the United States of commitments it has
> assumed in relations with the USSR and show
> that the American administration disregards
> the interests of the positive development of
> Soviet-American cooperation.

This followed the Soviet interpretation that peaceful
coexistence held between states of different social
systems and could not legitimately be linked to the
class struggle in the developing countries, of which
Afghanistan was an example. This divisibility of
detente was evident in a Tass statement on Carter's
speech (Pravda Jan. 7, 1980):

> It was apparently not by chance that the
> President said nothing about European affairs,

60

about a region where the trends in favour
of detente and mutually advantageous
cooperation among states with different
social systems have been developing quite
strongly and fully in the past few years.

The Soviet Union was pleased with the progress of
detente in this area.

It was also pleased with its progress in terms
of the class struggle, albeit this was precisely the
American objection to Soviet practice. Andropov dismissed US complaints and charged that the US was
undermining detente, using Afghanistan as an excuse.
The reasons for the switch in US foreign policy "lie
in the US ruling circles' fear of the wave of social
changes and in their desire to return the world to the
'blessed days' of imperialist domination". He held
that such changes lay in "the objective course of
history" and not "because the United States has not
taken proper cognizance of certain things in certain
places and has let opportunities slip in other
instances" (Pravda Feb. 12, 1980). This continued the
theme of the correlation of forces, shifts in which
underlay detente: to fight against this development
was, in the Soviet understanding, to fight against
detente.

Brezhnev also charged that such "anti-Soviet
hysterics" were not based on Soviet action in
Afghanistan. Rather he held that the American reaction to improved relations in Europe, to conclusion of
the Helsinki conference, "and to the victory of the
revolutionary peoples of Angola and Ethiopia over the
interventionists and mercenaries of imperialism" was
to delay ratification of SALT II, "encourage Sadat's
betrayal", "impose" on NATO an arms build-up and
deploy American missiles in Europe. In short, "the
present US leadership is pursuing a line aimed at
undermining detente" (Pravda Feb. 23, 1980). The
Americans were reacting adversely to these developments in the correlation of forces, unlike their

previous realistic acceptance of such changes.
Brezhnev stated that (<u>Pravda</u> Jan. 13, 1980):

> The deliberate aggravation of the inter-
> national situation caused by American
> imperialism expressed its displeasure with
> the consolidation of the positions of
> socialism, the upsurge of the national-
> liberation movement, and the strengthening
> of forces that favour detente and peace.

The American attitude towards changes in the correlation of forces and hence detente had changed which in
Soviet interpretation marked an illegitimate return
to the cold war: emphasizing the "objective" nature
of such developments, the Soviets denied responsibility for the worsening of inter-state relations as
alleged by the US.

Conclusion:

Based on radically different ideas concerning
the balance of power and the correlation of forces
respectively, the American and Soviet understandings
of detente concerning the Third World and military
intervention there were too dissimilar to permit
formulation of a rule of the game. The "debate" was
then predictable. The US held that the Soviet Union
violated the code of detente by intervening in Angola,
Ethiopia and Afghanistan; the Soviet Union denied
this and considered such action as supporting detente
by supporting the class struggle in the Third World.
On the other hand, American sanctions related to
detente, military intervention in Zaire and military
deployments and plans after Afghanistan ran contrary
to the Soviet conception of detente, by violating the
state-to-state agreements between the US and the USSR
and by fighting against the progressive forces in the
Third World, a form of neocolonialism. The US
considered such sanctions and counter-moves to be

perfectly legitimate within detente: the former
responded to Soviet violations, while the latter
fitted in with balance of power conceptions. This
exchange did little more than to deepen mutual dis
trust.

Detente arguably did not change Soviet-
American relations in the Third World: competition
certainly was not reduced or restrained within
mutually-agreed upon rules. However an important
feature of this period was American self-restraint
and Soviet lack of it in terms of military intervention, both direct and indirect. This did not arise
due to agreement, but did indicate that the game of
detente was played much more along Soviet lines than
along American ones at least until Afghanistan. The
Soviet interventions and lack of American response,
with the limited exceptions of Angola and Zaire,
corresponded to the favourable correlation of forces
and US recognition of this more than to maintenance
of the balance of power. Neither the US nor the USSR
was willing to link issues such as bilateral trade and
strategic arms negotiations to events in the Third
World, again at least until Afghanistan. This fitted
with the Soviet conception of the divisibility of
detente.

To what extent Afghanistan marks a change
from this remains to be seen: both sides interpreted
it as such a change. The Carter Doctrine is
supported by a Rapid Deployment Force which is not
yet operational: the US may or may not demonstrate
the capacity and willingness to play the balance of
power game by resorting to direct military intervention. The sanctions announced by Carter may or may
not stick: the grain embargo has been lifted, a
review of high technology exports to the USSR by the
West will be made, and strategic or theatre nuclear
arms negotiations are to resume. It appears
unlikely that the Reagan Administration will play the

detente "game" as it was played before Afghanistan, but it is not certain to what degree both the linkage of issues and the maintenance of the balance of power will be pursued. The possibilities of the game changing in these respects are certainly present.

4. STATUS QUO

The preceding discussion about the Soviet and American understandings of detente coupled with their respective conceptions of the correlation of forces and the balance of power revealed deep differences between these. The Americans stressed the legitimacy of the status quo, particularly in terms of the stability of Third World regimes. The Soviets stressed the legitimacy of changes in the status quo in the sense of gaining new clients in the newly-liberated countries. This resulted in a lack of agreement on the meaning of detente.

However, viewed from another perspective, the Soviet and American practice of military intervention may be sufficiently close that a rule of the game can be inferred from it. Although differing in size and duration, and interpreted by both sides in terms of supporting or changing the status quo ante, all of these interventions were responses to what the intervening patron considered to be threats to a Third World client. Furthermore, there were only military counter-measures by the other superpower when it considered its own clients or interests to be threatened in turn by the first state's intervention. The two states disagreed on the question of the legitimacy of supporting the status quo in the Third World. But on the basis of mutual self-restraint there was a rule of the game such that each permitted changes in the status quo ante unless these changes threatened each one's clients or vital interests.

Angola:

Both the US and the USSR interpreted the
Soviet intervention as changing the status quo ante
in Angola. In particular, the US considered the
Soviet action to threaten the American client in the
country. It therefore launched an indirect counter-
intervention.

The Soviet Union intervened both directly and
indirectly to support its protégé, the MPLA. Arms
supplies were resumed to it in October 1974 apparently
in response to Chinese and Zairean supplies to the
FNLA. Roberto's attacks on the MPLA in Luanda in
June and July 1975 were repulsed due to increased
Soviet shipments in March and April. The coalition
government agreed on at Alvor, Nakuru and Mombassa
was defunct, and the Soviet press commentary began to
reject the FNLA and UNITA as legitimate members of the
government (Pravda July 18, 1975). At this point the
Soviet Union may have intended to back the MPLA
sufficiently to put it in power alone, although the
option of a coalition government was retained should
the military or diplomatic situation require this.
Cuban advisers arrived in Brazzaville in July and in
Angola by August; some 1,500 Cuban troops had
arrived in Angola by the end of September. This may
have been related to concern for South African operations in the south, but also was to organize MPLA
units better and enable them to use the sophisticated
artillery they had received. The major deployment of
Cubans was at least in part in response to the SA
intervention in October. So the Soviet Union and Cuba
reacted to perceived threats to and opportunities for
their client.

The American reply was to authorize in July a
covert operation to supply the FNLA and UNITA with
arms: it was only at this time that the Ford Administration understood that the Soviets were equiping
the MPLA so as to completely defeat the FNLA, the
American client up to that time. Kissinger argued

66

(Senate 1976a:48) that the intervention was not intended to result in a complete defeat of the MPLA but to counter Soviet support, and so maintain a local balance of power. However Robert Ellsworth, Deputy Secretary of Defense, doubted that sufficient support was sent to the MPLA's opponents to ensure a "military stalemate" but that trained troops would have been required to offset the Cubans (73). As remarked above, the US was not willing to maintain the balance by direct military intervention.

The Ford Administration defended the operation on grounds of preserving the balance in southern Africa and countering Soviet moves so as to reassure allies. Robert Ingersoll, Deputy Secretary of State, briefed the Senate Subcommittee on African Affairs in July 1975 on aid to the FNLA and UNITA saying that this was required as a bargaining chip with the Soviets so as to make negotiations for a settlement possible (Bender 1978:96). In November Joseph Sisco, Undersecretary of State, and William Colby, the CIA Director, repeated this argument in requesting a tenfold increase in arms support to Zaire, holding that the balance of power must be maintained in Africa as elsewhere (New York Times Nov. 7, 1975). Following the House vote against the requested appropriations, Ford wrote to the Speaker, Carl Albert, citing the Administration's objections to the vote (DSB 1976a: 182):

> The US cannot accept as a principle of
> international conduct that Cuban troops and
> Soviet arms can be used for a blatant inter-
> vention in local conflicts, in areas
> thousands of miles from Cuba and the Soviet
> Union, and where neither can claim an historic
> national interest. If we do so, we will send
> a message of irresolution not only to the
> leaders of African nations but also to United
> States allies and friends throughout the world.

Kissinger voiced the same objection to the cut, noting that (DSB 1976a:8):

America's modest direct strategic and
economic interests in Angola are not the
central issue. The question is whether
America maintains the resolve to act
responsibly as a great power.... A stable
relationship with the Soviet Union based
on mutual restraint will be achieved only
if Soviet lack of restraint carries the risk
of counteraction.

Congress was criticized for preventing the Administration from playing the game at all.

The balance of power theme dominated other
considerations. Gulf Oil was prepared to deal with
the MPLA and only under pressure from the State
Department did it stop paying royalties to the movement. The CIA concluded that ideologically there
were no great differences between the three groups:
as Colby testified before the House Committee on
Intelligence in December 1975, support to Roberto and
Savimbi was desired purely to offset the Soviet role.

The US considered the Soviet-Cuban intervention to be an illegitimate challenge to the balance of
power in southern Africa and in Angola. In contrast
and in keeping with their understanding of the correlation of forces, Brezhnev remarked at the XXVth CPSU
Congress (Pravda Feb. 25, 1976):

In the developing countries, as everywhere
else, we are on the side of the forces of
progress, democracy and national independence
and regard them as our friends and comrades
in the struggle.

The MPLA victory represented a favourable development
in the correlation of forces. The Soviet press
criticised the US reaction to the intervention (Pravda
May 14, 1976):

US diplomacy does all it can to backup
reactionary anti-popular juntas--such as

the fascist junta in Chile--and thinks this
is 'legitimate'. At the same time, a
terrific hue and cry is raised about 'expansion' when the forces of progress assist
freedom-loving peoples subjected to aggression
by imperialism and racism. This is a clumsy
attempt to put into effect what Americans call
a 'double standard', an endeavour made with
unclean hands.

This suggested how such patron-client relations were
similar, while stressing the class-based legitimacy
of Soviet actions as opposed to American ones.
Arbatov noted US "dissatisfaction" with the reversals
in Angola and Vietnam (Pravda April 2, 1976):

After all, such defeats are related primarily
to the fact that the US invariably came to
the defense of notoriously unjust and doomed
causes. The blame for this rests with
vestiges of the cold war and its character-
istic bellicose anticommunism.

Defense of the status quo ante was both illegitimate
and bound to fail, as in Angola and Vietnam.

The Soviet Union intervened in Angola in order
to enable the local progressive forces to take power.
The United States responded to maintain the balance of
power locally and regionally. In particular, the US
interpreted the Soviet intervention to threaten the
American clients in Angola. Neither accepted the
legitimacy of the other's action.

The Horn:

The Soviet-Cuban direct intervention in
Ethiopia which began in November 1977, and had been
preceded by arms supplies which may not have arrived
until September, enabled the Somali army to be

defeated in the Ogaden in February and March 1978, and subsequently helped Mengistu regain control over Eritrea and Tigre. However Soviet support for the Derg was not unambiguous. The USSR had armed Somalia since 1963 and continued to do so until August 1977. Given the deterioration of the Derg's position during the summer, Soviet supplies and troops were slow in arriving although by March 1978 10,000 Cuban troops were deployed. The Soviet priority appears to have been to maintain relations with both Barre and Mengistu: Castro's proposal for a federation of the Horn was intended to prevent a split, and the USSR only intervened directly following the November break with Somalia. Only having lost this degree of diplomatic manoeuvre, were the Soviets prepared to cast in their lot with Mengistu. On his subsequent visit to Moscow he thanked his hosts "for their decisive support and internationalist assistance to the Ethiopian revolution in this struggle" (Pravda April 7, 1978).

Under the Ford Administration, Schaufele had noted the strategic importance of the "entire littoral" of the Horn and that it was American policy to prohibit local dominance by any one state, so as to keep the sea lanes open (Senate 1976:132). This justified American arms supplies to the Derg in order to balance Soviet shipments to Somalia. But the Soviet intervention in November 1977 occurred in a changed situation. The American reaction under Carter continued themes familiar under Kissinger but with far less vigour. Before the introduction of Cuban troops, Shulman expressed the Administration's view that the supply of arms in both Angola and the Ethiopia-Somalia war "contributed to local conflicts in a way that seriously destabilized the region" (DSB 1978 (Jan.):5). Carter criticised the Soviet Union for arming both Ethiopia and Somalia and thereby fuelling their conflict (DSB 1978 (Feb.):21). After the intervention of Cuban combat units Vance deemed these unacceptable as they raised the level of conflict, threatened the independence of African states, and created concern

70

among "moderate" African leaders that such interventions can be used "to determine the outcome of any dispute on the continent" (Senate 1978:7).

Vance indicated various means to counter such moves. These included public and private warnings to the USSR and Cuba, indications to the Soviets of the "dangers... for our overall relationship", the use of investment and aid in Africa so as to play to American economic strength, the support of peaceful changes in southern Africa so as to preclude Soviet and Cuban involvement, and "in exceptional circumstances" the transfer of arms (4-8). This was considered for Somalia by Vance in July so as to balance the Soviet buildup in Ethiopia (DSB 1977:169). But this offer was withdrawn in light of Somali military involvement in the Ogaden.

So the Carter Administration continued to think in at least some of the categories of balance of power strategy. The US emphasized the instability generated by Soviet actions. The Administration was concerned for the effect which this would have on African allies in terms of confidence in the US. Particularly under Andrew Young's influence, African affairs were seen in less strictly bipolar terms. But to the extent that diplomatic and economic means of influence were intended to curtail Soviet advances, the "game" continued to be played albeit with an unwillingness to intervene militarily either directly or indirectly.

The Soviet direct intervention, which revealed an impressive airlift capability, illustrated once again what a shift in the correlation of forces meant. It changed the status quo ante in a strategic sense: Ethiopia was confirmed as a Soviet client, and Somalia moved into the American camp. The Soviet navy eventually gained bases at Dahlak and Perim off the Eritrean coast, while losing Berbera to the Americans. Ethiopia became the strongest military power in the region. However the legal status quo ante was maintained: the Derg remained in power and Ethiopia was not dismembered under the pressures of Eritrean seccessionism and Somali irredentism. Concerned about African reactions, the US Administration acted on the latter by not intervening in the conflict: concern for the legal rules of the game outweighed concern for the strategic status quo.

However there were verbal agreements to limit the impact of the intervention, in the sense of not threatening Somalia, in return for American non-intervention. Vance reported that the Soviet Union had assured the US that Ethiopia would not invade Somalia if the US were to persuade Somalia to withdraw the WSLF from the Ogaden. The US refused to arm Somalia while its troops operated there. If Ethiopia however did cross the border, the Administration would reconsider its policy of non-intervention, which included prohibiting the sale of American arms by third parties such as Saudi Arabia and Iran to Somalia (New York Times February 11, 1978). David Aaron, US Deputy Assistant for National Security Affairs visited Addis Ababa on February 18 and 19, 1978. Mengistu then assured him that the Ethiopians would not enter Somalia if the US in turn assured Mengistu that it would not supply Somalia with arms. Visiting Mogadiscio on February 20 to 22, Gianni Giadresco, a senior official of the Italian Communist Party, assured Barre that the USSR wanted a negotiated settlement and would respect Somalia's borders. It is doubtful that Ethiopia had any interest in invading Somalia: rather Mengistu and the Soviets wanted to be sure of continued American non-intervention, and to do this they gave the US and Somalia reassurances that they would not threaten the new American client.

In contrast to Angola, there were greater constraints on unlimited Soviet support to Ethiopia in the sense of attacking Somalia. The Ethiopian-Somali conflict resembled the Middle East more than did the other three cases: as an inter-state conflict, the legal norms to be violated were clearer than in

Angola. Also, stronger Saudi, Iranian and American counter-intervention could be expected than the US and South Africa could provide in Angola, the former being restricted by domestic opposition and the latter by diplomatic isolation. The balance of power differed in the two cases.

The US permitted the Soviet-Cuban intervention in the sense of not counter-intervening even indirectly, although it considered that intervention to be illegitimate in terms of stability on the Horn. However the intervention did not change the status quo ante to the extent of threatening the new American client in the region and thus of altering the balance of power so radically as to exclude the US from the Horn. To this extent the US acquiesced to it in its policy of non-intervention.

Zaire:

The American role in the Shaba interventions continued their long standing support for Mobutu who had become particularly important after Haile Selassie's fall. American involvement in Angola was defended on grounds of reassuring leaders such as he, and Mobutu was instrumental in engaging Kissinger's attention in the conflict. Economic interest, particularly in minerals, and good political ties along with Mobutu's "constructive role in OAU and African councils" were cited in defending such substantial requests in military sales credits, totalling $40 million in 1978 (House 1977:195).

Mobutu's accusation of foreign involvement in Shaba was aimed at those states with the largest stake in his continuation in power and sensitive to instability due to an alleged Soviet-Cuban threat (Mangold 1979:109-112). Carter noted that domestic support was lacking to send a military force to Zaire in Shaba I although he supported the French, Moroccan and Egyptian response (DSB 1977:539). The Administration also approved Zaire's request for spare parts and other military equipment worth $2 million sent in an emergency airlift (New York Times March 16, 1977). Vance defended granting the request before the House Committee on International Relations, citing the "dangerous situation" for Zaire's copper industry created by the FLNC incursion (New York Times March 17, 1977). The US subsequently sent $13 million of "nonlethal" equipment, such as clothing and batteries; however the Deputy White House press secretary Rex Granum stated that the Administration did not consider the situation to be one of East-West conflict (New York Times April 13, 1977). Anthony Lake subsequently stated that in Shaba "we learned that the United States does not necessarily have to become fully involved on one side when some Soviet weapons are being used on the other" (DSB 1977:845).

Soviet commentary interpreted the action as supporting the status quo in terms of American economic and strategic interests (Pravda March 31, 1977):

> The ruling circles of the United States... exploited a purely internal conflict in Zaire as a pretext for intervening and expanding their influence in Zaire, taking into account both its natural resources... which are concentrated in Shaba province, and its strategic position (the center of Africa is also the rear support area of the 'front-line states'). It would be well to remember that American investments in Zaire are close to $1 billion.

So although the United States did not consider itself to be playing the balance of power game, the Soviet interpretation was consistent with this.

The United States had considered it appropriate to play this relatively small role in stabilizing

74

the situation. The Soviet-Cuban intervention in the
Horn came in between Shaba I and II such that the
latter required a show of resolve to friendly states
such as Egypt, Saudi Arabia and Zaire (Mangold 1979:
109). Carter indicated in the 1978 Annapolis speech
that the Administration's concern was along these
lines (DSB 1978 (July):16):

> We are deeply concerned about the threat
> to regional peace and to the autonomy of
> countries within which these foreign troops
> seem permanently stationed. That is why I
> and the American people will support African
> efforts to contain such intrusion, as we
> have done recently in Zaire.

The US did not wish to infringe the legal rules of the
game by intervening in the Horn. But the Shaba
intervention could only be interpreted as a reaffirma-
tion of support for Mobutu. The Soviet condemnation
of American involvement in Shaba II continued themes
prevalent in the first one. Support for Mobutu was
contrasted with Soviet support for Angola and
Ethiopia: the former stemmed from Western countries'
"own narrow and selfish interests" (Pravda June 23,
1978). Both the US and the USSR intervened to aid
African clients, but the former to maintain the
status quo ante and the latter to change it. There
were no Soviet military counter-moves to either Shaba
I or II. The USSR did not indicate that it considered
any of its own allies to be threatened by the two
interventions.

Afghanistan:

The Soviet intervention in Afghanistan can be
interpreted in terms of the status quo in two senses.
It maintained it in the sense of keeping Afghanistan
as a Soviet ally and continuing the PDPA regime,
albeit this involved a change in the government. However, it changed it in the sense of introducing Soviet

military units into an area in which they had not been
before, sufficiently close to the Persian Gulf to be
seen as a strategic threat by the US.

The first interpretation indicates that where
Soviet relations with clients are already established,
the USSR can become a status quo power in the Third
World, as it is in Eastern Europe. Ponomarev noted
that the states of socialist orientation must take
seven measures for their security, indicating Soviet
concern for this (1980:44). (i) The revolutionary
party must be guided by scientific socialism. (ii) It
must strengthen "the organs of democratic rule" and
(iii) form party and state cadres. (iv) A national
armed forces, "capable of defending the gains of the
people" must be built up. (v) Party and state ties
with the masses must be increased. (vi) A "correct"
social and economic policy must be pursued. (vii) These
states must develop relations with the socialist
commonwealth. In Afghanistan, the PDPA had failed to
fulfil a number of these tasks.

The Soviet intervention of December 1979 can
be interpreted as defending the status quo ante. The
PDPA faced a growing insurgency which was capable of
controlling substantial areas of the countryside,
although not the main cities. This in itself would
not be sufficient to topple the Soviet allies. But
desertions from the Afghan army and mutinies by
individual garrisons threatened to further loosen the
PDPA's control over the country, and this was beyond
the means of a Soviet indirect intervention, in the
form of arms and advisers, to control.

Furthermore, the USSR had reasons to desire
Amin to be deposed. Selig Harrison in interviewing
him found him to be more independently-minded than the
other pro-Soviet Afghan leaders (New York Times Jan.
13, 1980). He opposed broadening the PDPA government
to include Karmal and the Parcham faction and refused
to modify the government reforms which were creating
such widespread unrest. As Demchenko (1980) acknowl-
edged in Kommunist, he had "discredited progressive

76

ideas". Apparently Taraki agreed on his September 1979 visit to Moscow to remove Amin, but the attempt backfired as Amin learned of the plot through Tarun, Taraki's military aide (Khalilizad 1980:155). The Soviets had to acquiesce temporarily in the change. Following the coup, Moscow complied with Kabul's request that the Soviet ambassador Puzanov be recalled: he had been close to Taraki and had protected some of his supporters following the September shoot-out, reportedly as well as having been involved in planning the attempt against Amin. Amin's statements on Iran did not reflect shifts in Soviet policy towards that country, although previously the PDPA had followed the Soviet line on such matters. He reportedly opposed greater Soviet direct intervention and control over the Afghan military, although twenty battalions of Soviet troops entered Afghanistan to protect Soviet bases in early November (Daily Telegraph Nov. 3, 1979). Amin refused to pay a visit to Moscow in November and requested a meeting with Zia in early December (Washington Post Feb. 14, 1980). The Soviet Union may have been concerned that it would be unable to control or influence Amin, in addition to concern about the PDPA's position in Afghanistan. To this extent the intervention resembled those in Eastern Europe, and reflected concern for the status quo in the sense of preserving the Soviet position.

Both the Soviet military deployment and their interpretation of the intervention suggest that this is why they intervened. Reserve units from Central Asia which were not trained for counter-insurgency were initially sent into Afghanistan. Newell (1981: 177) has argued that this suggests that the Soviets intended only to control the cities and if necessary neutralize Afghan army units loyal to Amin. Their subsequent use of first-line troops, primarily of Slav composition indicates that they only later decided to adopt an active anti-insurgency role, given continued desertions from the Afghan army.

Soviet commentary stressed defending revolutionary gains--in this context, defending the

Soviet-PDPA position (*Pravda* Dec. 31, 1979):

> The Soviet Union believed that the imperialist
> forces, as they became convinced of the
> irreversibility of the changes taking place
> in Afghanistan, would not go beyond a certain
> limit but would reckon with reality. At the
> same time, our country made no secret of the
> fact that it would not allow Afghanistan to
> be transformed into a staging ground for the
> preparation of imperialist aggression against
> the Soviet Union.

The "revolution" was not to be defeated either by
insurgency or diplomacy. Commenting on the latter,
Kobysh noted that (*Literaurnya gazeta* March 12, 1980):

> The 'neutralization' label conceals a course
> aimed at the elimination not only of the
> government now in power in Afghanistan but
> also of the very system established by the
> Afghan revolution. This is why the presence
> of a limited contingent of Soviet troops in
> Afghanistan is arousing such rage in Washington,
> Peking and certain other capitals.

Brezhnev affirmed that (*Pravda* Oct. 17, 1980):

> The revolutionary process in Afghanistan is
> irreversible. The Afghan people and their
> government have on their side the support
> and solidarity of the Soviet Union and the
> other socialist states and of progressive
> forces the world over.

However American criticism of the intervention
was directed at its import for regional stability and
US security interests. This was not directed at the
situation within Afghanistan. Carter in his State of
the Union Address stressed "the implication of the
Soviet invasion of Afghanistan" which included a threat
"to the free movement of Middle East oil" and drew the
warning of the Carter Doctrine for the Persian Gulf

(DSB 1980 (Feb.):A-C):

> An attempt by any outside force to gain
> control of the Persian Gulf region will be
> regarded as an assault on the vital interests
> of the United States of America, and such an
> assault will be repelled by any means neces-
> sary, including military force.

The Soviets had to be penalised for the intervention
in Afghanistan so as to remove "the temptation to move
again and again until they reached warm water ports or
until they acquired control over a major portion of
the world's oil supplies" (DSB 1980 (March):34). It
was the prospect of further advances that drew an
adverse American reaction to the intervention in terms
of the regional status quo. The American response
would include additional military and economic aid to
Pakistan, negotiation for "facilities" in northeast
Africa and around the Gulf, and the establishment of a
Rapid Deployment Force so as to give the US the
capacity to intervene directly in the region.

A _Pravda_ editorial criticised Carter's
address and challenged the right of the US to declare
areas to be "spheres of America's 'vitally important'
interests" (Jan. 29, 1980):

> The message and the speech, permeated with
> a cold war spirit, openly state that the US
> claims to be a 'leading role in the world'.
> What 'leading role' means is Washington's
> intention to dictate its system in any
> region and to any state, and, when the US
> administration deems it expedient, to use
> any means, including weapons, to oppose
> national-liberation, revolutionary and all
> progressive movements. Thus, what we see
> here is a new American claim to world
> supremacy.

The American reaction was more in line with the
balance of power philosophy than had its reactions to

the Horn and Shaba been.   The Soviet Union understood
this and objected to it, contrasting it to its own
role of supporting the progressive forces.   It recognised without considering legitimate American concern
for regional stability (Pravda Dec. 31, 1979):

> Holes were found [following the fall of the
> Shah] in the notorious 'strategic arc' that
> Americans have been building for decades
> near the Soviet Union's southern borders....

But Ponomarev denied that American concern was well-
founded (Pravda Feb. 5, 1980):

> The events in Afghanistan in no way affect
> the state interests of the US. Incidentally,
> no one in Washington has dared to explain to
> Americans just what specific national inter-
> ests of the US are affected in Afghanistan,
> a subject on which the press and official
> circles are demagogically ranting.

The Soviets emphasized only the defensive aspects of
their intervention.

Some members of the Carter Administration
shared this view.   In explaining Soviet intentions to
the House Committee on International Affairs, Shulman
only included the considerations internal to
Afghanistan (House 1980:35-36). Vance and other
members of the Administration repeatedly stated that
one cannot "determine with certainty Soviet intentions
in the region--whether their motives in Afghanistan
are limited or part of a larger strategy".   It was
simply "prudent" to respond to this "potential threat"
and support American friends in the region (DSB 1980
(April):12).   The Carter Administration then seems to
have accepted both interpretations of the Soviet
intervention--that it supported the status quo in
Afghanistan but threatened it, intentionally or not,
in the region.   In terms of the first aspect, there is
no evidence of American military support to the Afghan

rebels--certainly not on a large scale. As the region was of great strategic importance, the US acted on the second interpretation. The Soviets certainly appeared to have gained the capacity both to threaten the flow of oil, by interdicting by air supplies passing through the Straits of Hormuz, and to become involved to a greater extent in Iranian and Pakistani internal politics. The American Rapid Deployment Force was set up in order to counter any Soviet intervention in Iran (Economist June 6, 1981:11). It is less clear that the Soviet Union intervened in Afghanistan with the intention of moving further towards the Gulf. The possibility nevertheless existed and the American reaction emphasized the change in the regional status quo brought about by the intervention.

Conclusion:

A rule of the game held between the US and the USSR on the basis of mutual self-restraint. This permitted military intervention by a superpower in response to what it considered to be a threat to one of its Third World clients from internal or external opposition, as long as this action did not in turn threaten the security of the other superpowers' clients or its vital interests. Only if the status quo ante was breached to this degree would the other power employ military means, including counter-intervention, as a sanction. In Angola, the Ford Administration replied in this way, although the Congressional opposition did not share this view. The Carter Administration reacted militarily to the Afghan intervention on the basis of its implication for the region, not for the conflict in Afghanistan. The Soviet Union considered military interventions which changed the correlation of forces in its favour to be legitimate, while the United States only considered interventions which preserved the balance of power to be acceptable. Nevertheless, a rule of the game related to this consideration operated on the basis of reciprocity.

5.   SPHERES OF INFLUENCE

        Some of the most often-cited rules of the game
concern the spheres of influence of the superpowers.
Vazquez (1973:301) defines such a sphere or zone as a
"space tacitly or expressly reserved to the hegemony
of one State". Tacit consent by other major states is
more likely. This may involve recognition of the
fact, if not the right, of local predominance. This
extends to permitting military intervention by a state
within its sphere in the sense of not counter-
intervening. Protest against the right of intervention
on legal grounds may follow, but local dominance is not
challenged with armed force. This does not however
preclude all diplomatic and economic ties between one
superpower and states within the zone of the other.

        Well-defined spheres of influence after World
War II are generally considered to exist in Latin
America and Eastern Europe. An American practice of
intervention in the former arose in Guatemala in 1954,
Cuba in 1961, and the Dominican Republic in 1965. Some
case can be made for continuation of this in Chile in
1973 and El Salvador in 1981. The Soviet practice
consists of the military interventions in Hungary in
1956, Czechoslovakia in 1968, and Poland in 1981. The
Monroe, Johnson and Brezhnev doctrines formulated the
claims of a right to intervene within each sphere.
Franck and Weisband (1970) have argued that on the
basis of reciprocity the latter two have established
norms of superpower intervention within their

respective spheres. Tacit consent to each other's
sphere is indicated by refraining from counter-
intervention.

A note of caution concerning tacit consent
is in order. A state may act so as to indicate such
consent without intending to do so. It is possible to
misinterpret such signals, particularly non-verbal.
No state is likely to announce that it has agreed to
such a division of areas. The US denied having done
so following the Warsaw Pact intervention in
Czechoslovakia (US Dept. of State 1968); but Soviet
"security interests" in Eastern Europe were explicitly
conceded by the Nixon Administration (President 1970:
55). Kissinger (1979:1151) interpreted the eleventh
principle of relations between the US and the USSR
(App. 13) concerning the renunciation of "special
rights or advantages in world affairs" as a repudia-
tion of the Brezhnev doctrine for Eastern Europe.
There is no indication that the USSR interpreted it as
such. So evidence for such consent could be contra-
dictory or ambiguous--the best case can be made on the
basis of consistent action.

These zones may also shift. As argued above,
the US generally sees these spheres as static, while
the Soviet Union sees these as changing in its favour.
Soviet relations with Cuba in military terms and--if
any--involvement in Nicaragua and El Salvador represent
at least some challenge to the American sphere. The
US has not however challenged the Soviet sphere in
Eastern Europe militarily.

It is more difficult to determine the existence of spheres of influence in the Third World: it
is possible to take a country's exclusion from
traditional American and Soviet spheres as a condition
for its inclusion in the Third World. However
criteria are available. The Soviet ones will be
considered below. American ones are more familiar.
They include "moderate", "democratic" or "anti-
communist" government, as determined by US Administrations, economic investment by private American

corporations, economic and military aid from the US
government, the distribution of regional security
responsibilities by the US as under alliances or less
formal arrangements, and finally a willingness to
assist client governments with military intervention
if necessary to withstand instability due to internal
or external opposition. Such contacts with either the
US or the USSR may be transitory: a switch from one
"camp" to another such as that of Egypt after 1972 and
Somalia after 1977 would be unlikely in Eastern Europe
and more difficult in Latin America. Finally, tacit
consent to the other state's contacts and in the last
resort military intervention indicate spheres of
influence, albeit these may be less well-defined than
in the traditional ones.

The questions then are: are the targets of
intervention within the intervening state's zone as
indicated by the above criteria? Was the fact of
local predominance conceded by the other state? Were
there any rules of the game for the US and the Soviet
Union based on these features?

Proletarian Internationalism:

An understanding of Soviet doctrine concerning
ties with Third World regimes and states is required
to determine the Soviet criteria for a sphere of
influence in the Third World. As Meissner has pointed
out, the doctrine of proletarian internationalism has
defined, albeit loosely, a sphere of influence within
which Soviet interventions are considered permissible
and appropriate in defense of socialist gains by the
USSR (1980:268-271). The states concerned are those
of socialist orientation, one of a growing number in
what the Soviets see as an increasingly well-defined
bloc.

States of socialist orientation are ones
which have achieved national liberation but not yet the

85

socialist revolution, and so shun capitalist methods
of development. They are in the intermediate stage of
the national democratic revolution, characterised by
three features: a non-capitalist path of economic
development is pursued, relations of broad co-operation
with and support from the socialist bloc are established, and the ruling "revolutionary-democrats"
gradually adopt Marxism-Leninism and organize themselves as vanguard parties. Tarabrin (1979:173) and
many other Soviet commentators have identified this
last one as the key feature of such states.

Eran has noted that these three conditions in
an earlier period constituted the Soviet equivalent of
influence (1979:129). Given favourable commentaries
by authors such as Kaufman (1979), Kosukhin (1979), and
Kim (1980:67) on these aspects in states including
Angola, Ethiopia and Afghanistan, the Soviets clearly
see these states within this category. Kim has
stressed that "further changes in the world balance of
forces played a tremendous role in strengthening the
social element of national liberation revolution" (69).
The revolutionary democrats are turning towards
scientific socialism and corresponding alignment with
the socialist bloc. He also indicated that with
increasingly bipolar social development, the Soviets
see a hardening of alignments within the newly-
liberated nations, with states such as the three
mentioned supporting the USSR in matters of foreign
policy and states such as Zaire, Egypt and Somalia
opposing it. It also demarcates more clearly areas in
which Soviet intervention is considered legitimate on
the basis of proletarian internationalism.

The principal Soviet sphere of influence is
considered to be Eastern Europe, as defined by the
Brezhnev doctrine and the practice of military intervention in Hungary in 1956 and Czechoslovakia in 1968.
The doctrine was not essentially new, but incorporated
the principle of the priority of the social over the
national revolution which had been clearly formulated
by the Soviet leadership as early as the 1920 Baku and
Moscow conferences, and was used to justify the

forcible retention of the "periphery" of the fledg-
ling Soviet state--maintaining as much of the
territory of the Russian Empire as possible. Thus
lacking an invitation from the Czechoslovak government,
the USSR argued that exercise of the right to national
self-determination so as to move out of the socialist
bloc "would run counter to Czechoslovakia's fundamental interests and would harm the other socialist
states". Support was therefore justified to prevent
"the export of counter-revolution from the outside".
To charge the Soviet Union with a violation of
Czechoslovak sovereignty indicated "a non-class
approach to the question" of self-determination (Pravda
Sept. 26, 1968). This right of intervention was an
important element in the relations of socialist internationalism between states of the bloc.

The claims for support to Angola, Ethiopia
and Afghanistan differ in that not being accounted
fully-fledged socialist states, the above principle
could not apply. Appeal could however be made on the
basis of the class principles of proletarian internationalism which oblige the socialist states, the
workers' parties and the national liberation forces to
solidarity and mutual support. Under these principles,
the Soviet Union has justified its interventions in
these three cases.

Angola:

In Angola, neither the US nor the USSR had a
strong basis on which to claim a sphere of influence.
Accordingly, the Soviet claim was challenged by the US
both in public statements and in the American indirect
intervention.

Both the Ford Administration and its Congressional opponents considered the Soviet Union to be
operating beyond its traditional sphere of influence.
Kissinger warned that failure to counter Soviet moves
would mean (Senate 1976b:493):

...that a pattern would be created in which countries would conclude that the Soviet Union, in places in which it had no historic interest, and Cuba, which had never operated outside the Western Hemisphere, would affect events without even financial opposition by the United States.

Senator Case noted that he and his Congressional colleagues were also concerned "that the Russians are exerting power so far away from their normal orbit" (Senate 1976b:500).

The Soviet Union contested this argument (Pravda Feb. 1, 1976):

But if we are speaking of historical interests, they exist not in the aspect the US Secretary of State has in mind but rather in the Soviet Union's full and consistent support of the people's struggle for freedom and independence.

Thus there was disagreement whether Angola lay within the Soviet sphere at the time.

The Soviet claim was partially true. As noted above, the relatively low level of support to the MPLA in the struggle against Portugal and Soviet defection from Neto to Chipenda cast some doubt on the "full and consistent" nature of the support. Soviet contacts with Neto stretched back to the early 1960s. At this time he established ties with the Portuguese Communists and with Alvaro Cunhal's aid travelled to Moscow in 1964. Cuba on the other hand had supported the MPLA consistently.

But Moscow was not the only power supporting the Angolan liberation movement. The Kennedy Administration had given aid to Roberto, although under Johnson this was reduced so as not to impair relations with Portugal, whose Azores airbase became increasingly important during the Vietnam war and under Nixon during

the 1973 Arab-Israeli war. Guided by NSSM 39 which
concluded that the Portuguese were secure in Africa,
the Nixon Administration further reduced this aid to
$10,000 a year. China had also been interested in
Roberto, inviting him to Peking in 1964 and 1968 and
supplying him with arms after his 1973 visit. The
Soviet criteria for a sphere of influence were only
partially fulfilled and not exclusively by the USSR.

One could however argue that the intervention
established such a sphere, particularly given American
unwillingness to intervene directly. This was
confirmed post facto by the inclusion of the MPLA into
the category of revolutionary democrats, and Angola as
a state of socialist orientation. This could be
accepted for the purposes of military intervention,
while recognising that the main American economic
interest in Angola, Gulf Oil in the Cabinda enclave,
was willing to deal with the MPLA throughout the civil
war and continued to do so amicably afterwards. In
Angola there was no agreement on a sphere of influence
and correspondingly both the US and the USSR supported
opposing sides in the conflict. However the introduction of Cuban troops, not matched by an American
response, established the subsequent Soviet claim to
such a sphere.

The Horn:

The situation in the Horn of Africa was complicated by the reversal of alignments. Yet the Soviet-
Cuban direct intervention only occurred when these
alignments had been redrawn, and amounted to a tacit
sphere of influence agreement.

Prior to the 1974 revolution in Ethiopia, the
American client was clearly Haile Selassie who received
military aid from 1949 to his fall as a rent for the
Kagnew communications centre. Ethiopia was considered
America's most valuable sub-Saharan African ally. The
Soviet Union became Somalia's arms supplier in 1963.

89

Following the 1969 military coup which brought Siad
Barre to power, these supplies increased, the Soviet
navy gained a base at Berbera, the Soviet Union and
Somalia concluded a treaty, and Barre was counted as
one of the revolutionary democrats in Africa.

Following the 1974 coup by the Provisional
Military Council or Derg, Ethiopia soon was included
within the group of states of socialist orientation.
(Izvestia Feb. 8, 1975). The Derg's programme of
April 1976 indicated that Ethiopia was embarked on
"the national-democratic revolution" whose goal was
"the socialist transformation of the country" (Pravda
May 16, 1976). Mengistu's rise to power helped to
improve relations (Ottaway and Ottaway 1978:166). He
was instrumental in the December 1976 arms agreement
which was conditional on cutting relations with the
United States. After his coup of February 3, 1977,
which the Soviets may have known of in advance given
the speed with which messages of support arrived, the
Declaration of Principles of Friendly Relations and
Cooperation marked "a qualitatively new character" in
relations. These were based on "historically established close bonds of friendship" and "the unity of all
progressive forces" (Pravda May 9, 1977). These
developments indicated that the Soviets considered to
have a stake in Ethiopia themselves.

For a period, the Ford and Carter Administrations challenged the growing Soviet position.
Schaufele held that the Derg's leaning to Moscow was
acceptable as it was short of "systematic opposition
to the United States" (Senate 1976c:121). The Ford
Administration would continue to supply Ethiopia with
arms due to the strategic importance of the Horn and
of the Kagnew base (113-4, 132). Under Carter, the
Military Assistance Program was stopped on grounds of
human rights violations by the Derg. But arms sales
were continued such that the total value of military
supplies received by Ethiopia from the US increased
following the 1974 coup. Talcott Seelye, Deputy
Assistant Secretary for African Affairs, explained that

continuation of support was intended to "help forestall a precipitate shift to Soviet and East European suppliers" (House 1977:193).

But the Administration did not compete far into 1977. The American decision to reduce the US military mission and the Kagnew base staff preceded the Ethiopian demand that these be closed (New York Times April 26, 1977). Non-military aid continued but the US conceded the role of arms supplier to the Soviets. The fact of Soviet preponderance in Ethiopia in this sense was thereby recognised.

The Soviets attempted to preserve their position in Somalia (Clark 1981:161-7). They did not conclude a treaty with Ethiopia, which would have indicated to the Somalis that ties with Ethiopia were considered to be on a par with those with Somalia. Castro's proposal in March 1977 for a federation of the Horn states and South Yemen, and Soviet proposals for a negotiated settlement (Pravda August 14, 1977) indicated a desire to avoid a rupture over the Ogaden issue. The Soviets were slow to deliver arms to Ethiopia. Little was sent after the December 1976 agreement. Many of the arms such as Mig 21s promised to the Derg in May 1977 did not arrive until September. The major air- and sea-lift of troops and equipment only began after the break with Somalia in November. The Soviets thereby conceded that Somalia was no longer in their camp.

Carter spoke of "peacefully challenging the Russians in their own spheres" in relation to both Ethiopia and Somalia in June 1977 (DSB 1977:3) and by July singled out the latter for an effort at realignment (DSB 1977:222). The Administration was aware of and supported earlier Saudi efforts to wean Somalia off the Soviet Union, and of Somali disenchantment with the Soviets (House 1977:194). Siad Barre visited Saudi Arabia in July, when he learned that the condition for $460 million of military aid was a total break from Moscow. This he was reluctant to do and only expelled a number of advisers before the November break.

This attempt on the part of the Saudis, with American approval, resembled the attempt by the Soviets in December 1976 to become the Derg's sole arms supplier. This encouragement to a local actor to expel the other superpower fits the pattern observed by Evron to be a rule of the Middle East game (1979: 23). The Horn was the case most similar to the Middle East in involving conflict between states and shifting alignments. This rule also distinguishes such cases from those involving states within the traditional Soviet and American spheres of influence.

The Soviet-Cuban intervention which began in November 1977 took place when the US had conceded that Ethiopia was in the Soviet camp and the USSR had conceded its position in Somalia to the US. This demarcation was further marked by the Soviet promise not to permit Ethiopian troops to enter Somalia, and the American undertaking not to arm Somalia unless it were attacked. The US consented to Soviet intervention in its newly-established sphere of influence. The Soviet Union agreed not to intervene beyond this. Despite the shift in alignments, Soviet and American action followed the rule of the game.

Zaire:

In the case of Zaire, there was no such complicating competition for influence. Girling has seen Zaire as the principal American client in black Africa after the fall of Haile Selassie, similar to Iran and Brazil in their respective regions (1980:127). Mobutu was instrumental in encouraging American support for Roberto during the Angola civil war. In that period the value of arms transfers rose from $1 million to $19 million. The value of arms sales credits peaked in 1977, before Shaba I, at $30 million out of a total of $62.5 million allocated for Sub-Saharan Africa. Private American investment in Zaire totalled nearly $1 billion, and the US depended substantially on copper and cobalt supplied by Zaire.

The Shaba II intervention indicated the American as well as the Belgian and French interest in Zaire. Airborne military intervention was also not a novelty: the Belgians in 1960, the Belgians and Americans in 1964, and the French and Moroccans in 1977 had set something of a precedent. The Soviets did not challenge this Western sphere, but were conscious of these ties as a form of "permanent intervention" (Pravda March 31, 1977). Zaire fitted into the "capitalist orientation" among the newly-liberated countries. The Shaba operation followed the rule.

Afghanistan:

Afghanistan had historically been either within the Russian orbit or at least contested by the Tsarist Empire as such. Russian rivalry with Britain marked periods of the nineteenth century in this buffer between the two empires, and was concluded in 1907 with an agreement that Afghanistan was not within the Russian sphere. In 1921 the new Soviet republic concluded a treaty with Afghanistan, from which time Soviet commentary dates relations on the basis of equality despite failure to live up to the treaty's provision to return the Panjeh which had been seized by Russia in 1885.

The Soviets had good grounds for considering the country to be within their sphere. In 1956, the Soviet Union became Afghanistan's main arms supplier following US rejection of Kabul's requests for military supplies. Mohammed Daoud was prime minister between 1953 and 1963 and during this period military and economic aid, trade and Soviet diplomatic support increased substantially. This was far greater than

93

American equivalents despite efforts under Zaher Shah's replacement for Daoud, Malwandwal, to seek funding from both the US and the USSR for the 1963-68 plan. The 1973 coup led by Soviet-trained officers which returned Daoud to power introduced an initial tilt towards the Soviet Union. This however swung back after 1975, when Kuwaiti, Saudi and Iranian economic aid was offered to Kabul to wean it away from its Soviet alignment. Daoud also dropped his border claims on Pakistan's North West Frontier Province.

It is not clear whether the Soviet Union was involved in the April 1978 coup: there is only circumstantial evidence. The coup was carried out by Soviet-trained officers organised by Amin, and executed at short notice when Daoud began arresting PDPA members. The officers handed control of the government over to the PDPA whose rival factions, Khalq and Parcham, had been reunited the previous year with Soviet mediation. The Soviet press greeted the change in power immediately and warmly, noting that Taraki had announced the beginning of the national democratic revolution (Pravda May 6, 1978). The Arab and Iranian offers were dropped and the border issue with Pakistan resumed. Increased trade and military assistance agreements were concluded with the USSR. Brezhnev and Taraki signed a treaty in December 1978, Brezhnev remarking that relations had assumed "a qualitatively different character" since the April revolution, these now being "permeated by a spirit of comradeship and revolutionary solidarity" (Pravda Dec. 6, 1978).

These developments eroded Afghanistan's claim to being non-aligned in any sense but the Soviet one, which takes the non-aligned movement and the socialist bloc to be "natural allies in the struggle for peace and against imperialism, capitalism and racism..." (Pravda Aug. 12, 1976). The Soviet criteria for a state of socialist orientation were clearly fulfilled before the December 1979 intervention, and on this basis lay the claim for a sphere of influence. The intervention, as it can be interpreted as supporting the status quo of the Soviet position in Afghanistan, can be interpreted as preventing Afghanistan from sliding out of the Soviet zone.

The Carter Administration reacted somewhat ambiguously to this situation. Carter criticised the December 1979 intervention partly on the grounds that it was the first use of Soviet troops outside of the Warsaw Pact since World War II. In Angola and Ethiopia they had employed "surrogates" (DSB 1980 (March):29). Although officials such as Brzezinski (1981:20) and Shulman (House 1980:61) conceded that Soviet influence had been preponderant in recent Afghan history, the latter held that the invasion was "a new departure". It differed from an application of the Brezhnev doctrine in going beyond the Soviet "primary security zone" in Eastern Europe.

The intervention in Afghanistan was signif-icant in these terms, but not to the extent that Carter tried to depict it. The Administration shared the Soviet perspective in distinguishing the inter-vention in Afghanistan from those in Czechoslovakia and Hungary. However it made more out of the distinc-tion between Afghanistan and the Soviet-Cuban inter-ventions in Africa than did the Soviets: "defense of socialist gains" does not require that any particular socialist state intervene, and only Soviet troops were positioned appropriately in the Afghan case. The East European interventions had both involved several member states of the WTO. The Soviets had staked out their claim in Afghanistan along the lines of those in Angola and in Ethiopia and indeed in clearer terms. Moreover, there are grounds for holding that the United States tacitly accepted this claim or at least that Moscow would have had reason to think so.

Throughout the post-war period, American interest in Afghanistan declined. US aid to Kabul between 1955 and 1965 was $350 million compared to $552 million from the USSR. The American total fell to $150 million between 1965 and 1977 and was further reduced after the killing of Ambassador Dubs in February 1979.

Theodore Eliot, Dubs' predecessor, interpreted the April 1978 coup as a move away from non-alignment (1979:57-60). Jack Miklos, Deputy Assistant Secretary for Near Eastern and South Asian Affairs, echoed this view in May 1979, remarking on "the degree of the Soviet presence in Afghanistan and the orientation of the Afghan's current foreign policy..." as new (House 1979a:24). He stated that the Soviet-Afghan treaty "can be interpreted to mean that the USSR would come to Afghanistan's aid if asked in a military way" (18).

On the other hand, the United States warned the Soviet Union not to intervene in Afghanistan on several occasions during 1979. In a diplomatic note sent in March the US stated that it would "regard external involvement in Afghanistan's internal problems as a serious matter with a potential for heightening tensions and destabilizing the situation in the entire region" (New York Times March 23, 1979). Brzezinski repeated the warning on August 2 and the State Department on September 20. On the 26th, Harold Saunders, Assistant Secretary of Near Eastern and South Asian Affairs, told the House Committee on Foreign Affairs that "we have repeatedly impressed on the Soviet Government the dangers of more direct involvement in the fighting in Afghanistan" (House 1979a:33). Shulman gave somewhat different evidence to the House Subcommittee on Europe, to the effect that the five communications in December with the Soviets were the first such warnings. He noted that Soviet responses to these were "unsatisfactory" but that they cannot have been in doubt about how seriously the US would view the situation (House 1980:111).

The Carter Administration conceded the fact of Soviet predominance while denying any related Soviet right to intervene, which the Soviets clearly thought they possessed in terms of a sphere of influence. Although this constitutes an instance in which the rule of the game is unclear, there are grounds to favour the Soviet interpretation. First the American signals were arguably confusing--the actions indicated a "retreat" from Afghanistan which may have led the

Soviets to discount the value of their warnings.
Second, there were no indications of American intent
to counter-intervene: they had not even done so to
save the Shah of Iran. Third, the American reaction
indicated concern not with Afghanistan itself but with
possible further moves: the Carter Doctrine for the
Persian Gulf indicated unambiguously that American
interests lay there, to be covered by an untested
declaration of a sphere of influence. Sanakoyev
voiced Soviet concern at this declaration of "national
interests", which "it should be noted, extend to all
parts of the world, particularly to regions close to
the borders of the Soviet Union and the other socialist
countries" (1980:85-7). The US objected to the intervention as far as it concerned Afghanistan primarily
on legal grounds. The Soviets would at the least have
good reason to interpret these as American concessions
that Afghanistan lay within Moscow's sphere as defined
by proletarian internationalism.

Conclusion:

        A number of conclusions can be formulated
regarding the rules of the game concerning spheres of
influence. First, Soviet-American rivalry, inasmuch
as it involved military intervention, was pursued outside of the two powers' traditional spheres of influence
in these four cases, indicating a rule based on mutual
self-restraint. Furthermore, what perhaps could be
termed secondary spheres of influence existed on the
basis of tacit consent in the Third World, and these
provided further rules. Second, each state unilaterally intervened within its own sphere: the
United States in Zaire and the Soviet Union in
Ethiopia and Afghanistan. The last intervention in
particular was intended to prevent Afghanistan from
moving out of the Soviet orbit, and to this extent
resembled Soviet action in Hungary and Czechoslovakia.
Third, each state respected the other's sphere by not
intervening and in particular by not challenging

militarily the other's interventions. Fourth, only
the Soviet-Cuban intervention in Angola was outside
of the zone of either power. But this was not
challenged by a comparable direct intervention by the
US and so laid claim to a Soviet sphere in Angola.
Fifth, the jockeying for allies on the Horn prior to
the Soviet-Cuban direct intervention indicated that it
was permissible for the two powers to encourage local
actors to expel the patron superpower so as to alter
zones of influence in the area--a rule not to be
found in superpower relations with their traditional
zones. Superpower competition in the Third World
was regulated to some degree by tacit agreements on
shifting or newly-established spheres of influence,
such that interventions within these were not
challenged militarily by the other power and intervention outside of a sphere, as in Angola, was rare and
did not risk such a challenge.

6. MILITARY CONFRONTATION

One concern about Soviet and American interventions in the Third World has been that a serious
military confrontation between the two could ensue.
It is important to consider if there were any rules
of the game which deal with this. On the basis of
explicit or tacit agreements or simply mutual self-
restraint, are there any patterns of action that
suggest that the US and the USSR only intervene under
conditions so as to minimize the risks of direct
military confrontation between them? There are two
possible rules of the game in this area besides others
such as agreements on spheres of influence which serve
the same purpose. First, the superpowers may only
intervene directly in a conflict when the risk of
direct counter-intervention by the other power is
small. Second, they may employ proxies or allies
whenever possible in direct interventions.

Counter-Interventions:

In all four cases, direct military intervention by one power ran no or negligible risks of a
direct counter-intervention by the other power. This
rule did not hold in terms of indirect intervention.
Outside of these cases, the Arab-Israeli conflict
alone provides plenty of examples of races between the
US and the USSR to build up their clients' arsenals.
This was also the case in Angola. Soviet arms

deliveries to the MPLA resumed in October 1974
apparently in response to Chinese supplies to the
FNLA. The US decided in July 1975 to arm the FNLA and
UNITA following the Soviet shipments to the MPLA in
the spring. But in terms of direct military intervention, the rule did hold in Angola.

The introduction of Cuban troops occurred
roughly in two stages. In September and early October
1975 approximately 1,500 were landed. This may have
been related to South African incursions into
southern Angola in August which mostly involved raids
against SWAPO camps, but it was probably required in
order to integrate Cuban troops with MPLA formations
so as to organize these more effectively and operate
the more sophisticated equipment, particularly artillery and tanks, then reaching the MPLA. The second
stage was in response to the South African intervention
which began in mid-October. This involved the deployment of Cuban troops on a much larger scale and also
involved full Soviet logistical and naval support for
the operation.

At no time did the United States indicate a
willingness to counter-intervene. The US did not
raise the matter with the Soviets until October, and
then reportedly urged them not to intervene but with
only the threat of an indirect, not a direct counter-
intervention. The US had the capacity to put a naval
blockade around Angola which probably would have cut
the supply of troops to Luanda. A task force was
assembled in the Azores around USS _Independence_ but
never sent to Angola. Soviet warships were deployed
off Gibraltar to counter this, and the US was not
willing to risk a naval confrontation over Angola--as
it had been over Cuba--so that US non-intervention
conformed to the rule. Kissinger indicated publicly
that the United States would not intervene beyond its
covert operation (_New York Times_ Nov. 29, 1975) and
there cannot have been much doubt about whether
Congress would permit this so soon after the collapse
of South Vietnam. On December 9 Ford proposed to

Dobrynin that all foreign military intervention and shipment of military equipment be ended. The Soviet airlift of troops and equipment then ceased until the Senate blocked the appropriations for the covert operation, when it was resumed at a higher level. In terms of the introduction of combat units, the Soviets intervened in a situation in which a commensurate American counter-intervention was unlikely.

In the Horn, American reluctance to become involved militarily soon surfaced. There had been no such interest in Shaba I in May 1977 when only "non-lethal" military supplies were sent to Zaire. In June and July, the Carter Administration showed interest in prying Somalia away from the Soviet Union, by becoming the source of military supply for Mogadiscio (DSB 1977:169, 229). Siad Barre's American physician Dr. Kevin Cahil reportedly passed messages to him concerning such intentions from Washington, and the Somalis claimed to have expected such support. But the US retreated from this position when it became clear that Somali troops were fighting in the Ogaden and concern was raised that the US would lose diplomatic support among African states. Young subsequently stated that Kenya had constituted the strongest opposition to it (House 1979b:24). On September 1 the State Department announced that the US would not supply Somalia with arms, nor allow third parties such as Iran or Saudi Arabia to do so. The ban remained in effect even after the Somali break with the USSR and the subsequent introduction of Cuban troops into Ethiopia. The United States indicated that it would only consider the Somali requests for arms if Ethiopian units crossed the border, and this the Soviets promised to prevent. At the time of the February 1978 counter-offensive, only three American destroyers were in the seas off the Horn, further indicating no desire to intervene.

The Soviets appreciated this reluctance. They first accused the United States of goading on Somalia and arming it, but later switched to noting that Barre had merely been promised such arms (_Izvestia_ Jan. 29, 1978). The press also condemned Saudi, Iranian and Egyptian efforts to dominate the Red Sea, holding that this was NATO's work but not accusing the US or other NATO members of direct involvement (_Pravda_ May 5, 1977). The Soviet-Cuban intervention beginning in November and December with the introduction of troops faced no likelihood of an American counter-intervention.

Similarly, the Shaba II intervention in March 1978 did not run any risk of a Soviet counter. Indeed as argued above, Soviet and Cuban involvement in the FLNC operation was probably minimal if anything at all and their denials of responsibility for this further indicated that they had no intention of becoming involved.

Afghanistan provoked American sanctions and the Carter doctrine. But there was no intention to counter the Soviet intervention directly with military means, and Carter's address to the nation indicated that military sanctions would not be used (DSB 1980 (Jan.):A-B). It was often argued that US failure to oppose Soviet military interventions in Angola and Ethiopia contributed to the Soviet calculation that the same would hold true in Afghanistan and when asked about this Carter was rather evasive (DSB 1980 (March): 8). Given what was argued above concerning the likely Soviet understanding of American signals, both sides took this as a further case of intervention running little or no risk of counter-intervention by the other superpower.

This was held in all four cases when direct as opposed to indirect military intervention has occurred. Arms build-ups by both sides to local clients occurred in Angola, but the Soviet-Cuban direct military intervention was not countered. In Angola and Ethiopia Cuban troops faced South African and Somali forces respectively. But in neither case did the United States support these forces or introduce its own. US non-intervention as in Angola indicated that one power would refrain from direct intervention if this carried a high risk of confrontation with the other one. Kaplan has concluded that this abstention from counter-intervention applies more widely (1981: 56-60). In no instance of direct confrontation had this been intended by either state. There has been a consistent pattern whereby American and Soviet interventions did not run a high risk of counter-intervention by the other state.

Proxies:

Only in Afghanistan were the combat troops introduced either Soviet or American. In Angola and Ethiopia, Cubans supplied the manpower although Soviet logistical support was essential. In Shaba II French and Belgian paratroops were flown in American transports which were required; the US also brought in the subsequent Moroccan and francophone African force. To call these troops "proxies" suggests that they serve the interests of the allied superpower and possibly also suggests that they are not involved for their own reasons. However, the states so involved as proxies had interests of their own to be so. It would then perhaps be more accurate to speak of a rule based on mutual restraint such that both the US and the USSR rely on allied forces for military interventions in the Third World whenever possible.

There are several reasons to regard Cuba as a relatively autonomous actor in Angola and not as a "puppet" without any interests of its own involved. First, it realized the Cuban leadership's desire to further the cause of revolution in the Third World by military means. This had failed in South America where the bourgeoisie was too strong, as Castro put it; but Africa lacked this feature and so provided more promising territory. Cuban involvement in Africa began in the early 1960s. Che Guevara had contacts with the MPLA and other national liberation groups in this period. Cubans began providing training to the

MPLA in Brazzaville in 1965 and the next year Neto visited Havana, after which Angolans received education and military training in Cuba. Elsewhere in Africa, a Cuban military mission was opened in Ghana in 1961, followed in the mid-1960s by ones in Congo-Brazzaville and Guinea, and by the mid-1970s there were military missions in six other African states.

The Angolan intervention also played a role in Cuban domestic politics. Kapcia (1979:157) has argued that it provided a means of mobilizing and enthusing the population for whom the revolutionary myths had faded. Ethiopia continued this role. Gonzalez (1977:3-9) has described how the decision to intervene in Angola resulted from a struggle within the expanded ruling élite. The factions in favour of revolutionary anti-imperialism--the "fidelista"--and in favour of sustaining military missions overseas to support Cuban foreign policy won, reflecting the increased strength since 1970 of Raul Castro and the Fuerzas Armadas Revolucionarias in decision-making. Valenta (1981:45) reported that it improved Cuba's bargaining position vis-à-vis the Soviet Union on aid and trade.

However, Cuban freedom of action was not unlimited in these matters. The Soviet rescue of the Cuban economy after the 1970 failure to achieve a ten million ton sugar harvest, and penetration of the Cuban security apparat after 1971 suggests that Soviet influence in Cuban decision-making was not negligible. The initial dispatch of about 250 advisers by July and 1,500 troops by October was done employing Cuban transports and may not have been planned in conjunction with the Soviet Union. However Soviet logistical support for the subsequent, larger intervention was required. If the USSR had wished to prevent the Cuban intervention, it could have done so. There are however some grounds for holding that Cuba initiated the Angolan operation.

There are however no grounds for this in the case of Ethiopia, suggesting that Cuban freedom of action was more restricted. Prior to 1977, Cuba did not have any contacts with the Derg, while Soviet contacts were established shortly after its ascendency to power in 1974. Indeed in pursuing its support for national liberation movements, the Cubans had provided arms and training to the EPLF in its guerrilla war against Addis Ababa. In March 1977 there were still Cuban advisers in Somalia, but not in Ethiopia. However at this time Castro accepted the Ethiopian view of a socialist-oriented federation on the Horn which would not involve the loss of Eritrea and the Ogaden as proposed by Barre. Castro hailed Ethiopia as Africa's first socialist state. So Cuba was moving along with the USSR in favouring Ethiopia, but probably following the Soviet lead. Although the Ethiopian foreign minister travelled to Havana on October 15, probably to request Cuban troops, these troops were deployed under Soviet command in the Ogaden. The Cubans reportedly refused to engage in combat in Eritrea (Selassie 1980:141-5). These facts suggest that Cuban intervention in the conflict in the Horn stemmed less from their own interests than did their intervention in Angola.

There is no conclusive evidence that Zaire and South Africa acted as proxies for the US in Angola. Zairean troops reportedly were deployed with the FNLA in mid-summer 1975 but it is not clear how many were involved nor for how long. Zaire's role was of greater importance as a source of supply for the FNLA. Zaire had its own reasons to be involved in the Angolan conflict. It wished to gain control over the oil-rich Cabinda enclave and supported the seccession movement there. Mobutu was suspicious of Soviet influence in the region, particularly via the MPLA. He had further worries for his security in the form of the ex-Katangese gendarmes in Angola, who triggered the Shaba incidents. Mobutu was therefore instrumental in developing and supporting the FNLA whose leader, Roberto, was his brother-in-law. Mobutu also requested US involvement in Angola following an alleged military coup against him early in 1975. Zaire clearly gained in terms of American military assistance which rose

enormously to a peak of $31 million in 1977. Zairean
involvement in the Angolan civil war preceded the
American intervention and indicated a large degree of
independence.

South Africa had reasons to intervene similar
to those of the US. SA intended to counter the Soviet-
Cuban deployment of arms and troops which by September
threatened to install an MPLA government. This was
regarded as a Marxist puppet, which could provide a
secure base for SWAPO and constitute an undesirable
development in the long term for SA, faced also with
the prospect of FRELIMO in Mozambique. The SA intervention was requested by Chipenda, Savimbi and
possibly Zaire and the Ivory Coast. SA hoped for US
support but appears to have been unaware of the extent
of its diplomatic isolation: in what it depicted as a
stand on behalf of the "free world" against "communism"
it received no overt American support, nor is there
any evidence of covert American diplomatic, economic
or military assistance. The South African intervention does not then count as an American one by proxy.

In Zaire, both Belgium and France had
substantial interests involved. Belgian assets in
the former colony were greater in value than American
ones, and the majority of Europeans in Kolwezi were
Belgians. France wished to extend its practice of
intervention to this the largest francophone African
state so as to gain closer relations with Mobutu.
Given Franco-Belgian disagreement over how to conduct
the 1978 operation, there may have been some competition in this quarter. The operation was timely for
the French as they were about to host a francophone
African summit dealing with military co-operation.
The French saw this as a unilateral operation:
François Poncet, the foreign minister, claimed that
the American transports were only required to speed
up the operation, and the previous one had not
required them (Manin 1978:160-3). The French and the
Belgians had their own reasons for intervening:
American ones were arguably symbolic in terms of
signalling to the Soviet Union, Cuba and African

states. The Carter Administration saw itself as "supplementing" and coordinating with France and Belgium in terms of arms supplies to and intervention in Zaire (Senate 1978:29). As in the Angola case for Cuba and the USSR, French and Belgian involvement preceded the American one, suggesting that this was a case of reliance on allies rather than a use of proxies.

Afghanistan constitutes an exception to the rule and so suggests that the qualification "if possible" is appropriate. A land-locked country adjacent to the Soviet Union, a Cuban expeditionary force would hardly have suited. Initially reserves with a high proportion of troops from the Central Asian republics were deployed in Afghanistan, to be replaced by largely Slav-composed units. Despite a different mix of nationalities, these all count as Soviet troops. But this would not appear to constitute an exception of great importance: it is not obvious that troops from other socialist states could have been used, and the switch from reserves to first-line units suggests to some degree a lack of preparation such that the most readily available units had to be deployed.

The cases indicate a pattern of mutual restraint whereby the US and the USSR rely on military forces from allied states for these interventions when this is possible. In every case with the probable exception of Ethiopia the allies concerned had their own reasons to intervene and were only proxies in the sense that their presence removed any requirement for American or Soviet combat--as opposed to logistical--units to be involved.

Conclusion:

These interventions exhibited patterns of mutual self-restraint so as to reduce the risk of

direct military confrontation between the superpowers.
Direct military intervention did not face the likelihood of counter-intervention directly by the other
power. Allied troops were employed in such direct
interventions whenever this was possible. This
suggests that considerations of relative power, and
the desire to avoid dangerous confrontations and
crises weighed in the thinking of Soviet and American
leaders.

7. REGULATED CONFLICT

The discussion has indicated that despite strong disagreements and violent action, there were rules of the game of superpower military intervention in the Third World in this period. Regulation of such international conflict operates at many different levels of formality and explicitness.

On a generalized level, Himes (1980:220) has indicated four areas of collective action to institutionalize permissible conflict in a society. The extent to which these areas are not covered in the rules of the game indicates the extent to which this process of formalizing rules has not developed--but this is not to deny that some results have not been achieved.

(1) There was a recognition of the divergent or incompatible interests of the parties involved. The US and the USSR saw themselves not as cooperating in the Third World but as competing for influence. Each tended to view the other as behind unfavourable developments, even if these were wholly or largely local.

(2) The parties agreed to guarantee each one's right to pursue these interests, limited by the other's right to do so as well. Here "right" does not convey any sense of consenting to the legitimacy of each one's interventions: the disagreements over the application of the legal rules, over their respective

conceptions of detente and over the maintenance of or change in the status quo in the Third World emphasized that American and Soviet leaders were deeply divided over the nature of legitimacy. But due to relative power and out of prudence each state permitted on a reciprocal basis the other's military interventions in the ways indicated.

(3) The parties established and enforced rules to regulate their conflict:

(i)   The consent of the government of the target state was required. This was accepted by both parties as a rule in all four cases but only respected in Ethiopia and Zaire. Quite apart from the legal question of recognition, these interventions cast doubt on the strength of indigenous support which these governments enjoyed. The norm permitting humanitarian intervention or rescue of nationals arguably depended on this norm of consent, and was subject to some controversy.

(ii)   Intervention must have been intended to counter aggression by a third party against the target state. Again, this was explicitly accepted as a legal norm in every case but only observed in one, that of Ethiopia, which was attacked by Somalia. This indicated the tendency for intervening states to emphasize the external aspects of internal conflicts in order to justify their own involvement.

(iii)   Based on their respective understandings of the balance of power and of the correlation of forces, the American and Soviet conceptions of detente in the Third World were too dissimilar to permit agreement on a rule of the game. However their practice indicated that there was little or no linkage between their competition in the Third World and their relations in other fields, at least until Afghanistan. Coupled with unilateral American self-restraint from direct, and to a large extent, indirect military intervention, in this period until Afghanistan the "game" of detente was played far closer to the Soviet conception of its "rules" than the American one.

(iv)   Underlying their different conceptions of detente, the US and the USSR disagreed as to whether military intervention in the Third World must preserve the status quo or not: the US argued that it must not disturb it while the Soviet Union in arguing that it could support the newly-emergent progressive forces in this manner held that interventions could ligitimately change the status quo. However on the basis of mutual self-restraint both sides accepted that intervention by one power to support its clients threatened by internal or external opponents was permissible, in the sense that the other power would not counter-intervene, unless the initial intervention threatened the clients or the vital interests of the other power.

(v)   There were tacit agreements on spheres of influence within the Third World, based on appropriate criteria for the US and the USSR. These interventions indicated that the two states conducted their military competition outside of their traditional spheres. Each one respected the other's sphere of influence even if this was newly-established as in the Horn. Each was permitted to exploit unilaterally its local predominance in this sense in Zaire, the Horn and Afghanistan, which in the last case involved preventing a state from sliding out of the intervener's zone. Angola was the only case of intervention outside of a superpower's sphere of influence, but it did not provoke a direct counter-intervention and so established a Soviet sphere there. Local actors in the Horn were encouraged by one superpower or its allies to expel the other one so as to change spheres of influence.

111

(vi)   On the basis of mutual self-restraint, there
        was a rule that direct interventions only
        occurred when there was little or no risk of
        direct counter-intervention by the other super-
        power. This would reduce the likelihood of a
        military confrontation.

(vii)   The Soviet Union and the United States employed
        allied troops whenever possible so as to reduce
        this risk. This occurred in every case except
        Afghanistan in which only Soviet troops could
        have been used.

        (4) An agency to supervise and enforce the
rules and arbitrate disputes about them--the last
feature cited by Himes--was not established. This
existed in the United Nations and to a lesser extent
in regional bodies such as the OAU and the Islamic
Conference. But their decisions were not accepted
when these ran contrary to the US objectives in Angola
and the Soviet one in Afghanistan. Such an agency in
any case only dealt with the legal rules. The other
rules which were established bilaterally were also
enforced on that basis by the threat of sanction and
maintained on a reciprocal basis. Conflict between
the superpowers does not require a Leviathan in order
for there to be rules binding on the two.

Basis of Agreement and Compliance:

        What considerations would lead to these rules
being chosen? Why were some respected, and others
infringed? Partial answers can be provided by
considering the factors enhancing maintenance of rules
of conflict as Deutsch has dealt with them (1973:379).

        (1) The rules are known. This was most
obviously true regarding the norms of law and of
detente inasmuch as both sides had signed the public
Basic Principles. Yet the former were often infringed
and no rule prohibiting intervention was derived from

the Principles. Tacit rules and patterns of mutual
self-restraint may then have been considered to be
well known by both Soviet and American leaders. This
suggests the importance of related verbal and non-
verbal signalling. However agreements concerning
spheres of influence may become more explicit, as
indicated by the conclusion of treaties between the
Soviet Union and Third World states.

(2) The rules are clear, unambiguous and
consistent. The explicit rules suffered on this
score. There were disagreements as to the legitimate
governments concerned and whether there was aggression
against the target of intervention. Soviet and American legal doctrine differed from other interpretations of the laws concerned. There was no agreement
on the meaning of the Basic Principles concerning
Third World interventions. In contrast, there was
little misunderstanding or disagreement on the non-
explicit rules with the possible exception of the
question of whether Afghanistan lay within the Soviet
zone or not.

(3) The rules are not perceived to be biased
against one's own interests. This held in all cases
of agreement on the rules. Although frequently
infringed, the legal norms agreed upon were sufficiently vague that they could be used by each state to
advantage in certain circumstances. Disagreements
over the rules--support for decolonization, detente
and the status quo--stemmed from this consideration.
In terms of influence, especially economic, in the
Third World the US is seen to be ahead of the USSR.
Thus the former wishes to preserve its generally
favourable position while the latter wishes to improve
its own using the tools with which it is best equiped:
military strength. By contrast, US detente policy
hoped for competition to be transferred to the
economic sphere, thus playing to American strength.
The rules by and large favoured superpower clients:
the MPLA, Mobutu, the Derg, and at least the Parcham
faction of the PDPA. They did not address the interests of other significant actors: the FLNC and other

opponents of Mobutu, the FLNA and UNITA after the MPLA
was established as the Angolan government, the
Eritreans and ethnic Somalis in the Ogaden, and
apparently the vast majority of Afghans. To the
extent that the interests of these actors were not
considered, there are grounds for holding the rules
to be unjust. But it was not assumed that the superpowers adopted these norms on moral criteria. To the
extent that they provided a modicum of order and
helped to avert major confrontations between the US
and the USSR, the rules served the interests of more
than just the superpowers and their clients.

(4) The other party adheres to the rules.
This condition obtained in the rules concerning
spheres of influence, support for local clients
threatened by instability, and military confrontations.
It did not in the legal ones which both sides
infringed. No absolute prohibition on intervention
could be established due to lack of this.

(5) Violations are quickly known to significant third parties. The United States and the Soviet
Union took legal arguments to the UN in the Angola and
Afghanistan cases, and in the Horn paid their verbal
respects to the OAU. The Soviet Union cited that
organization's condemnation of the French and American
proposal for an African interventionary force, and the
US the Islamic Conference's condemnation of the Soviet
invasion of Afghanistan. With their bilateral rules,
third parties concerned tended to be allies in NATO or
the Warsaw Pact, or in the Third World, be they
"moderates" or "revolutionary democrats". In such cases
whether there had been a violation depended on each
side's understanding of the rule in question, and so
appeal went to allies who shared much the same interpretation.

(6) There is significant social approval for
adherence and significant social disapproval for
violations. The legal norms tended to have diplomatic
sanctions as in the UN resolution condemning the Soviet
intervention in Afghanistan, and OAU criticism of the

Shaba interventions. But the legal sanctions were infrequently applied and were not very effective. The Soviet Union's support to Angola and Ethiopia was approved of by the OAU. During this period, American unilateral restraint failed to induce any comparable Soviet restraint. The Americans applied detente-related sanctions after Afghanistan: their failure to do so previously suggested that they did not consider the purported rule prohibiting Soviet interventions to be of greatest importance in the detente relationship and arguably signified consent to the Angolan and Ethiopian cases. For the other rules there was no approval beyond tacit consent, but direct military confrontation with the other superpower, or the toppling of one power's clients by the other would be the sanctions applicable to these rules. Soviet and American leaders by implication regarded these as more significant sanctions than the legal ones available: the rules rested on considerations of relative power and willingness to employ this.

(7) Adherence to the rules has been reward-ing in the past. These rules have been employed in previous situations, as has been treated in the relevant literature. Few of these earlier cases dealt with Third World interventions. With the exception of the Middle East, they were based on American practice in Latin America and Soviet practice in Eastern Europe. Only detente was new and this failed to generate any new rules. But it was incorrect to draw the conclu-sion from the detente debate that there were no rules of the game in the Third World. Rather the same or similar rules which had obtained in other areas were continued by the US and the USSR. The rules concern-ing spheres of influence, avoidance of the risk of counter-intervention by the other superpower, and the employment of allied troops contributed to what had long been a central concern of Soviet-American rela-tions: the avoidance of confrontations which could lead to a nuclear war. The Basic Principles made this concern explicit and it was respected. The Soviets and Americans failed to conclude an explicit under-standing concerning the spirit of detente. Nevertheless

its central feature was agreed upon in the Principles and complied with tacitly on the basis of these previously-established rules.

(8) One would like to be able to employ the rules in the future. Given their value in the past, the rules can be expected to continue in the future albeit changes are not impossible. In particular the failure of the American policy of detente to generate mutual self-restraint in Third World military interventions has been fully appreciated and may lead to a return to action consistent with the balance of power thinking which underlay detente but which was not carried out fully in action. As the nature of the game changes, so will the rules. The period chosen was marked by a degree of retrenchment in American interventions, and of expansion in Soviet ones. Different policies of intervention by either or both powers could change the rules.

Other actual or potential interventionary situations exist: El Salvador and Poland in the respective zones of the US and the USSR, continuing Middle East conflicts concerning both Arab-Israeli relations and the Persian Gulf, or further unrest in Angola and the Horn, as well as the guerilla war against South Africa. The cases considered have not involved China: perhaps there are similar rules of the game of Sino-Soviet competition in South-East Asia. The rules should have some predictive value, in indicating where and in what circumstances intervention is likely, although lack of a direct Soviet intervention in Poland in 1980-81 and American refusal to support Somoza in Nicaragua and the Shah in Iran in 1979 show that the rules alone are not sufficient for this purpose. An examination of such instances in which intervention did not take place would be required to reveal what other factors are taken into consideration, along with the role of the rules in prohibiting intervention.

Complete pessimism regarding superpower conflict in the Third World is not supported by this

116

discussion: rules did regulate this conflict in its most violent and potentially dangerous form, military intervention. But nor is complete optimism warranted: there were significant weaknesses in the rules. None dealt with the limitation of violence in Third World conflicts unless this was required to protect super-power interests. Reflecting this, there was no rule prohibiting superpower intervention, and the restraints on indirect intervention were fewer than those on direct intervention. Coupled with the limited consideration of interests of all but a few Third World actors, the rules fail to provide much hope for them. The rules also do not guarantee that direct superpower military confrontation will be avoided. Miscalculation of risks, misunderstanding of signals and over-reaction to threats to interests could upset that pattern of largely indirect competition observed in these four cases whereby only one power intervened directly in each case. Further-more, neither side shared the other's sense of legitimacy. Detente was not based on any shared values beyond mutual desire to reduce the risks of nuclear war. The distrust of this period may result in more confrontational military action by either the US or the USSR. Despite these rules, the future, if not apocalyptic, does not look safer or more peaceful.

RELEVANT PROVISIONS OF

THE CHARTER OF THE UNITED NATIONS

Article 2.

(4) All members shall refrain in their international relations from the threat or use of force against the territorial integrity or political independence of any state, or in any other manner inconsistent with the purposes of the United Nations.

. . . .

(7) Nothing contained in the present Charter shall authorize the United Nations to intervene in matters which are essentially within the domestic jurisdiction of any State or shall require the Members to submit such matters to settlement under the present Charter; but this principle shall not prejudice the application of enforcement measures under Chapter VII.

. . . .

Article 51.

Nothing in the present Charter shall impair the inherent right of individual or collective self-defence if an armed attack occurs against a Member state, until the Security Council has taken measures necessary to maintain international peace and security. Measures taken by Members in the exercise of this right of self-defence shall be immediately reported to the Security Council and shall not in any way affect the authority and responsibility of the Security Council under the present Charter to take at any time such action as it deems necessary in order to maintain or restore international peace and security.

U.N. General Assembly Resolution 2225(XX),
December 21, 1965

Declaration on the Inadmissibility of Intervention
in the Domestic Affairs of States and the Protection
of Their Independence and Sovereignty

The General Assembly,

Deeply concerned at the gravity of the international
situation and the increasing threat to universal peace
due to armed intervention and other direct or indirect
forms of interference threatening the sovereign personality and the political independence of States,

Considering that the United Nations, in accordance
with their aim to eliminate war, threats to the peace
and acts of aggression, created an Organization, based
on the sovereign equality of States, whose friendly
relations would be based on respect for the principle
of equal rights and self-determination of peoples and
on the obligation of its Members to refrain from the
threat or use of force against the territorial integrity or political independence of any State,...

...Recognizing that full observance of the principle
of the non-intervention of States in the internal and
external affairs of other States is essential to the
fulfilment of the purposes and principles of the
United Nations,

Considering that armed intervention is synonymous with
aggression, and, as such, is contrary to the basic
principles on which peaceful international co-operation
between States should be built,

Considering further that direct intervention, subversion and all forms of indirect intervention are

contrary to these principles and, consequently, constitute a violation of the Charter of the United Nations,

Mindful that violation of the principle of non-intervention poses a threat to the independence, freedom and normal political, economic, social and cultural development of countries, particularly those which have freed themselves from colonialism, and can pose a serious threat to the maintenance of peace,

Fully aware of the imperative need to create appropriate conditions which would enable all States, and in particular the developing countries, to choose without duress or coercion their own political, economic and social institutions,

In the light of the foregoing considerations, solemnly declares:

    1. No State has the right to intervene, directly or indirectly, for any reason whatever, in the internal or external affairs of any other State. Consequently, armed intervention and all other forms of interference or attempted threats against the personality of the State or against its political, economic and cultural elements, are condemned.

    2. No State may use or encourage the use of economic, political or any other type of measures to coerce another State in order to obtain from it the subordination of the exercise of its sovereign rights or to secure from it advantages of any kind. Also, no State shall organize, assist, foment, finance, incite or tolerate subversive, terrorist or armed activities directed towards the violent overthrow of the regime of another State, or interfere in civil strife in another State.

    3. The use of force to deprive peoples of their national identity constitutes a violation of their inalienable rights and of the principle of non-intervention.

4. The strict observance of these obligations
is an essential condition to ensure that nations live
together in peace with one another, since the practice
of any form of intervention not only violates the
spirit but also leads to the creation of situations
which threaten international peace and security.

5. Every State has an inalienable right to
choose its political, economic, social and cultural
systems, without interference in any form by another
State.

6. All States shall respect the right of
self-determination and independence of peoples and
nations, to be freely exercised without any foreign
pressure, and with absolute respect for human rights
and fundamental freedoms. Consequently, all States
shall contribute to the complete elimination of racial
discrimination and colonialism in all its forms and
manifestations.

7. For the purpose of the present Declaration, the term "State" covers both individual States
and groups of States.

8. Nothing in this Declaration shall be
construed as affecting in any manner the relevant
provisions of the Charter of the United Nations
relating to the maintenance of international peace
and security, in particular those contained in
Chapters VI, VII, and VIII.

U.N. General Assembly Resolution 3314 (XXIX),
April 12, 1974

The Definition of Aggression

The General Assembly,

...

Adopts the following definition:

Article 1

Aggression is the use of armed force by a State
against the sovereignty, territorial integrity or
political independence of another State, or in any
other manner inconsistent with the Charter of the
United Nations, as set out in this definition.

Article 2

The first use of armed force by a State in contravention of the Charter shall constitute prima facie
evidence of an act of aggression although the Security
Council may in conformity with the Charter conclude
that a determination that an act of aggression has
been committed would not be justified in the light of
other relevant circumstances including the fact that
the acts concerned or their consequences are not of
sufficient gravity.

Article 3

Any of the following acts, regardless of a declaration
of war, shall, subject to and in accordance with the
provisions of article 2, qualify as an act of aggression:

> (a) The invasion or attack by the armed forces
> of a State of the territory of another State,

or any military occupation, however temporary, resulting from such invasion or attack, or any annexation by the use of force of the territory of another State or part thereof;

(b) Bombardment by the armed forces of a State against the territory of another State or the use of any weapons by a State against the territory of another State;

(c) The blockade of the ports or coasts of a State by the armed forces of another State;

(d) An attack by the armed forces of a State on the land, sea or air forces, marine and air fleets of another State;

(e) The use of armed forces of one State, which are within the territory of another State with the agreement of the receiving State, in contravention of the conditions provided for in the agreement or any extension of their presence in such territory beyond the termination of the agreement;

(f) The action of a State in allowing its territory, which it has placed at the disposal of another State, to be used by that other State for perpetrating an act of aggression against a third State;

(g) The sending by or on behalf of a State of armed bands, groups, irregulars or mercenaries, which carry out acts of armed force against another State of such gravity as to amount to the acts listed above, or its substantial involvement therein.

...

Article 5

No consideration of whatever nature, whether political, economic, military or otherwise, may serve as a justification for agression.

A war of aggression is a crime against international peace. Agression gives rise to international responsibility.

124

No territorial acquisition or special advantage resulting from aggression are or shall be recognized as lawful.

...

Article 7

Nothing in this definition, and in particular article 3, could in any way prejudice the right to self-determination, freedom and independence, as derived from the Charter, of peoples forcibly deprived of that right and referred to in the Declaration on Principles of International Law concerning Friendly Relations and Co-operation among States in accordance with the Charter of the United Nations, particularly peoples under colonial and racist régimes or other forms of alien domination; nor the right of these peoples to struggle to that end and to seek and receive support, in accordance with the principles of the Charter and in conformity with the above-mentioned Declaration.

U.N. General Assembly Resolution 3328 (XXIX),
December 16, 1974

Implementation of the Declaration on the Granting
of Independence to Colonial Countries and Peoples

The General Assembly,

. . .

5. Reaffirms its recognition of the legitimacy
of the struggle of the peoples under colonial and
alien domination to exercise their right to self-
determination and independence by all means at their
disposal, and notes with satisfaction the progress
made by the national liberation movements of the
colonial Territories, particularly in Africa, both
through their struggle and through reconstruction
programmes, towards the national independence of
their countries;

. . .

7. Urges all States and the specialized agencies
and other organizations within the United Nations
system to provide moral and material assistance to all
peoples under colonial and alien domination struggling
for their freedom and independence, in particular to
the national liberation movements of the Territories
in Africa, in consultation, as appropriate, with the
Organization of African Unity;

. . .

APPENDIX 5

U.N. Security Council Resolution 387 (XXXI), March 31, 1976

The Security Council,

...

Recalling the principle that no State or group of States has the right to intervene, directly or indirectly, for any reason whatever, in the internal or external affairs of any other State,

Recalling also the inherent and lawful right of every State, in the exercise of its sovereignty, to request assistance from any other State or group of States,

Bearing in mind that all Member States must refrain in their international relations from the threat or use of force against the territorial integrity or political independence of any State, or in any other manner inconsistent with the purposes of the United Nations,

Gravely concerned at the acts of aggression committed by South Africa against the People's Republic of Angola and the violation of its sovereignty and territorial integrity,

...

1. Condemns South Africa's aggression against the People's Republic of Angola;

2. Demands that South Africa scrupulously respect the independence, sovereignty and territorial integrity of the People's Republic of Angola;

...

4. Calls upon the Government of South Africa to meet the just claims of the People's Republic of Angola for a full compensation for the damage and destruction inflicted on its State and for the restoration of the equipment and materials which its invading forces seized;

...

APPENDIX 6

U.N. General Assembly Resolution ES-6/2,
January 14, 1980

The Situation in Afghanistan and its Implications

for International Peace and Security

The General Assembly,

. . .

1. Reaffirms that respect for the sovereignty,
territorial integrity and political independence of
every State is a fundamental principle of the Charter
of the United Nations, any violation of which on any
pretext whatsoever is contrary to its aims and purposes;

2. Strongly deplores the recent armed intervention in
Afghanistan, which is inconsistent with that principle;

3. Appeals to all States to respect the sovereignty,
territorial integrity, political independence and
non-aligned character of Afghanistan and to refrain
from any interference in the internal affairs of that
country;

4. Calls for the immediate, unconditional and total
withdrawal of the foreign troops from Afghanistan in
order to enable its people to determine their own form
of government and choose their economic, political and
social systems free from outside intervention, subversion, coercion or constraint of any kind whatsoever;

. . .

APPENDIX 7

Relevant Provisions of the Charter of

the Organization of African Unity

We, the Heads of African States and Governments
assembled in the City of Addis Ababa, Ethiopia:

...

Determined to safeguard and consolidate the hard-won
independence as well as the sovereignty and territorial integrity of our States, and to fight against
neo-colonialism in all its forms;

...

Principles Article III

The Member States, in pursuit of the purposes stated
in Article II, solemnly affirm and declare their
adherence to the following principles:

...

3. Respect for the sovereignty and territorial
integrity of each State and for its inalienable right
to independent existence.

O.A.U. AHG/Res. 72/(XII), August 1, 1975

On the Situation in Angola

The Assembly of Heads of State and Government of the
O.A.U.,

...

Deploring the bloody confrontations between the
principal Liberation Movements and the non-respect by
the signatories of the Agreements of Kinshasa,
Mombassa, Alvor and Nakuru,

Convinced that it is the duty of O.A.U. to seek, by
every means, to restore peace, harmony and understanding in Angola, in particular before the date of the
proclamation of independence scheduled for 11 November
1975:

1. Urgently appeals to all Liberation Movements to
lay down their arms;

2. Earnestly requests Portugal to assume, without
delay and in an impartial manner, its responsibilities
in Angola;

...

APPENDIX 9

O.A.U. AHG/Res. 85/(XIV), July 5, 1977

On Interference in the Internal
Affairs of African States

The Assembly of Heads of State and Government of the
Organization of African Unity meeting in its Fourteenth
Ordinary Session held in Libreville, Gabon, from 2 to 5
July 1977,

...

1. Recommends that Member States exert every effort
so that, in respecting the O.A.U. Charter, they may
safeguard their identity and remain outside conflicts,
especially ideological conflicts, emanating from without the African continent;

2. To this end, urgently calls on all African States
so that, without prejudice to their right to conclude
defence agreements of their choice intended especially
to forestall outside aggressions, they refrain from
having recourse to foreign intervention in the settlement of conflicts between African States;

3. Calls on all extra-African powers, particularly
the big ones, to refrain from interfering in the
internal affairs of African States;

4. Further calls on Member States to prohibit the use
of their territories as base for political subversive
activities against another African State as well as

the maintenance and the establishment of foreign
military bases on their territories, and requests them
to liquidate the foreign military bases existing on
the African continent;

5. Recalls, in this context, that the interference in
the internal affairs of States poses grave threats to
international peace and security since it creates
favourable conditions for questioning the personality
and the values on which African States repose;

6. Strongly emphasizes that the situation thus created
is prejudicial to the stability and development of
African States;

7. Calls on African States to refrain from harbouring,
financing and using nationals of neighbouring countries
against their countries of origin.

APPENDIX 10

O.A.U. CM/Res. 635/(XXXI), July 15, 1978

On an Inter-African Military Force of Intervention

The O.A.U. Council of Ministers:

...

Conscious of the inalienable right of every State to take any measures it deems necessary to safeguard its sovereignty, freedom and independence, and protect its security;

...

Considering the attempt by non-African powers to threaten the peace and security of the African continent under the pretext of establishing an inter-African collective security force:

1. Affirms that Africa's defence and security are the exclusive responsibility of the Africans;

2. Solemnly declares that the creation of an inter-African force can be envisaged only within the context of the O.A.U.'s objectives and priorities for the elimination of the racist minority regimes of Southern Africa, the total liberation of the continent, and the safeguarding of the independence, sovereignty and territorial integrity of Member States;

3. Calls for the reactivation of the O.A.U. Defence Commission to consider the desirability of establishing an Inter-African Military Force under the aegis of the O.A.U.;

4. Appeals to all Member States to settle their disputes by peaceful means, including recourse to the O.A.U. Commission of Mediation, Conciliation and Arbitration.

APPENDIX 11

O.A.U. CM/Res. 641/(XXXI), July 15, 1978

Measures to be taken against Neo-Colonialist
On Military Interventions in Africa and on
Manoeuvres and Interventions in Africa

The O.A.U. Council of Ministers:

...

Seriously concerned with the policy of interference,
aggression, intervention and the encouragement of
expansionism by external forces of domination and
exploitation against the states and peoples of Africa,
especially since the collapse of the Portuguese
colonial empire;

Seriously alarmed by intrusion of the number of foreign
powers in various parts of the continent and their
relentless effort to create or perpetuate conflicts
and artificial divisions and sow disunity so as to
check the momentum of solidarity and the African
people's desire for unity;

...

1.   Strongly denounces the policy of force, interference from any source whatsoever against Africa to
recolonize the continent;

2.   Condemns all initiatives and actions which
contravene the principles and objectives of the Organization and encourage attempts at dominating and
dividing Africa;

3. <u>Declares</u> that peace and security of African states are contingent upon strict adherence to the principles of people's right to self-determination and independence and of non-interference, territorial integrity, inviolability of frontiers, non-recourse to the use of force and non-recognition of territorial acquisition by use of force, and that differences should be settled by peaceful means and within an African context;

4. <u>Draws</u> Member States' attention to the dangers to the peace and security of the whole continent by pacts that encourage interference and military intervention and hamper the liberation process of peoples;

5. <u>Solemnly declares</u> that, in all cases, the security of Africa is the concern of Africans only and that no power or group of powers outside Africa is to interfere in this respect;

6. <u>Reiterates</u> its firm condemnation of the tendency of certain non-African powers to use mercenaries against the security, independence and sovereignty of African States and to establish their domination and maintain a climate of tension and conflict in the continent;

7. <u>Reaffirms</u> its will to work towards the elimination of foreign military bases and to oppose all power blocs and divisionist policies.

Soviet-Afghan Treaty of Friendship,
Good-neighbourliness and Co-operation
December 5, 1978

The Union of Soviet Socialist Republics and the
Democratic Republic of Afghanistan,

Reaffirming their commitment in the aims and
principles of the Soviet-Afghan Treaties of 1921 and
1931, which laid the basis for friendly and good-
neighbourly relations between the Soviet and Afghan
peoples and which meet their basic national interest,
...
Being determined to develop the social and economic
achievements of the Soviet and Afghan peoples, to
safeguard their security and independence and to come
out firmly in favour of the unity of all the forces
fighting for peace, national independence, democracy
and social progress,
...
Attaching great importance to the further strengthening
of the contractual-legal basis of their relations,

And _reaffirming_ their devotion to the aims and
principles of the United Nations Charter,

Have decided to conclude the present Treaty of Friendship, Good-neighbourliness and Co-operation and have
agreed on the following:

Article 1

The high contracting parties solemnly declare their
determination to strengthen and deepen the inviolable
friendship between the two countries and to develop
all-round co-operation on the basis of equality,

respect for national sovereignty, territorial integrity
and non-interference in each other's internal affairs.
...

Article 4

The high contracting parties, acting in the spirit of
the traditions of friendship and good-neighbourliness,
as well as the United Nations Charter, will consult
each other and by agreement take appropriate measures
to ensure the security, independence and territorial
integrity of the two countries.
        In the interests of strengthening their
defence capacity the high contracting parties will
continue to develop co-operation in the military field
on the basis of appropriate agreements concluded
between them.

Article 5

The Union of Soviet Socialist Republics respects the
policy of non-alignment which is pursued by the
Democratic Republic of Afghanistan and which is an
important factor for maintaining international peace
and security.
        The Democratic Republic of Afghanistan
respects the policy of peace pursued by the Union of
Soviet Socialist Republics and aimed at strengthening
friendship and co-operation with all countries and
peoples.

Article 6

Each of the high contracting parties solemnly declares
that it will not join any military or other alliances
or take part in any groupings of states, or in action
or measures directed against the other high contracting
party.

...

APPENDIX 13

Basic Principles of Relations between
the United States of America and
the Union of Soviet Socialist Republics

May 29, 1972

The United States of America and the Union of Soviet
Socialist Republics,
...
Have agreed as follows:

First. They will proceed from the common determination that in the nuclear age there is no alternative
to conducting their mutual relations on the basis of
peaceful coexistence. Differences in ideology and in
the social systems of the U.S.A. and the U.S.S.R. are
not obstacles to the bilateral development of normal
relations based on the principles of sovereignty,
equality, non-interference in internal affairs and
mutual advantage.

Second. The U.S.A. and the U.S.S.R. attach major
importance to preventing the development of situations
capable of causing a dangerous exacerbation of their
relations. Therefore, they will do their utmost to
avoid military confrontations and to prevent the outbreak of nuclear war. They will always exercise
restraint in their mutual relations, and will be
prepared to negotiate and settle differences by
peaceful means. Discussions and negotiations on out-
standing issues will be conducted in a spirit of
reciprocity, mutual accommodation and mutual benefit.

Both sides recognize that efforts to obtain unilateral advantage at the expense of the other, directly

or indirectly, are inconsistent with these objectives.
The prerequisites for maintaining and strengthening
peaceful relations between the U.S.A. and the U.S.S.R.
are the recognition of the security interests of the
Parties based on the principle of equality and the
renunciation of the use or threat of force.

Third. The U.S.A. and the U.S.S.R. have a special
responsibility as do other countries which are
permanent members of the United Nations Security
Council, to do everything in their power so that
conflicts or situations will not arise which would
serve to increase international tensions. Accordingly,
they will seek to promote conditions in which all
countries will live in peace and security and will not
be subject to outside interference in their internal
affairs.

. . .

Eleventh. The U.S.A. and the U.S.S.R. make no claim
for themselves and would not recognize the claims of
anyone else to any special rights or advantages in
world affairs. They recognize the sovereign equality
of all states.

The development of U.S.-Soviet relations is not
directed against third countries and their interests.

Twelfth. The Basic Principles set forth in this
document do not affect any obligations with respect to
other countries earlier assumed by the U.S.A. and the
U.S.S.R.

BIBLIOGRAPHY

Adomeit, Hannes. (1973) Soviet Risk-Taking and
    Crisis Behaviour. Adelphi Paper no. 101.
    London: I.I.S.S.

Africa Contemporary Record (1976-1980) New York:
    Africana Publishing.

Akehurst, Michael. (1977) "The Use of Force to
    Protect Nationals Abroad". International
    Relations 5: 3-23.

Albright, David E. (ed.) (1980) Communism in Africa.
    Bloomington: Indiana University Press.

Arbatov, G.A. (1973) "On Soviet-American Relations".
    Kommunist no. 3 in Survival 15: 124-129.

Aspaturian, Vernon V. (1980) "Soviet Global Power
    and the Correlation of Forces". Problems of
    Communism 29 (no. 3): 1-18.

_____. (1980) "Moscow's Afghan Gamble". The New
    Leader 63 (no. 2): 7-13.

Ayoob, M. (1979) "The Superpowers and Regional
    'Stability': Parallel Responses to the Gulf
    and Horn". World Today 35: 197-205.

_____. (ed.) (1980) Conflict and Intervention in
    the Third World. London: Croom Helm.

141

Beitz, Charles. (1979) Political Theory and Inter-
     national Relations. Princeton: Princeton
     University Press.

Bell, Coral. (1977) The Diplomacy of Detente. London:
     Martin Robertson.

Bennouna, Mohammed. (1974) Le Consentement à l'ingé-
     rence militaire dans les conflits internes.
     Paris: Librairie Générale de Droit et de
     Jurisprudence.

Bender, Gerald. (1978) "Kissinger in Angola: Anatomy
     of a Failure". In René Lemarchand (ed.)
     American Policy in Southern Africa: the Stakes
     and the Stance. Washington: University Press
     of America.

Bertram, Christoph.(ed.) (1980) Prospects for Soviet
     Power in the 1980s. London: I.I.S.S.

van der Beugel, Ernst. (1980) "Coping with the After-
     math of Afghanistan". Survival 22: 242-247.

Bissel, Richard E. (1978) "Southern Africa: Testing
     Detente". In Grayson Kirk and Nils H. Wessell
     (eds.) The Soviet Threat: Myths and Realities.
     New York: Praeger.

Blechman, Barry M. and Kaplan, Stephen S. (1978)
     Force Without War: U.S. Armed Forces as a
     Political Instrument. Washington: The
     Brookings Institute.

Bowett, Derek W. (1974) "The Interrelation of
     Theories of Intervention and Self-Defense" in
     Moore.

Brezhnev, Leonid. (1978) in Survival 20: 32-35.

_____. (1979) Peace, Detente and Soviet-American
     Relations. New York: Harcourt, Brace,
     Johanovich.

Brownlie, I. (1963) International Law and the Use of Force by States. Oxford: Clarendon Press.

Brutents, K. (1979) "The Soviet Union and Newly-Independent Countries". International Affairs (Moscow) no. 4: 3-14.

Brzezinski, Zbigniew. (1979) in Survival 21: 180-181.

_____. (1981) "A Long Conversation With...." Encounter 61 (no. 5): 13-30.

Bull, Hedley. (1977) The Anarchical Society: A Study of Order in World Politics. London: MacMillan.

Cervenka, Zdenek and Legum, Colin. (1978) "Cuba: The New Communist Power in Africa". Africa Contemporary Record 1977-78. New York: Africana Publishing.

_____. (1980) "The Organization of African Unity in 1978: The Challenge of Foreign Intervention". Africa Contemporary Record 1978-1979. New York: Africana Publishing.

Chaffetz, David. (1980) "Afghanistan in Turmoil". International Affairs 56: 15-36.

Clark, Ian. (1981) "Soviet Arms Supplies and Indian Ocean Diplomacy". In Larry W. Bowman and Ian Clark (eds.) The Indian Ocean in Global Politics. Boulder, Co.: Westview Press.

Cohen, Raymond. (1979) Threat Perception in International Crisis. Madison: The University of Wisconsin Press.

_____. (1980) "Rules of the Game in International Politics". International Studies Quarterly 24: 129-150.

Cohen, Raymond. (1981) "'Where are the Aircraft
        Carriers?' - Nonverbal Communication in Inter-
        national Politics". Review of International
        Studies 7: 79-90.

Coplin, W.D. (1965) "International Law and
        Assumptions About the State System". World
        Politics 17: 615-634.

Current Digest of the Soviet Press.

D.S.B. see U.S. Department of State. Bulletin.

Dahm, H. (1976) "The Ideological Background of the
        25th Congress of the C.P.S.U. in View of
        Foreign Policy". Studies in Soviet Thought
        16: 103-111.

Davis, Nathaniel. (1978) "The Angola Decision of
        1975". Foreign Affairs 57: 109-124

Deane, M.J. (1976) "The Soviet Assessment of the
        'Correlation of World Forces': Implications
        for American Policy". Orbis 20: 625-636.

De Lima, F.X. (1971) Intervention in International
        Law. The Hague: Uitgerverij Pax Nederland.

Demchenko, P. (1980) "Afghanistan: Standing Guard
        over the People's Gains". Kommunist no. 5:
        71-78 (J.P.R.S. 75780).

Deutsch, Morton. (1973) The Resolution of Conflict.
        New Haven: Yale University Press.

Donaldson, Robert H. (ed.) (1981) The Soviet Union in
        the Third World: Successes and Failures.
        Boulder, Co.: Westview Press.

Ebinger, Charles K. (1976) "External Intervention in
        Internal War: The Politics and Diplomacy of
        the Angolan Civil War". Orbis 20: 669-699.

The Economist (June 6, 1981) "Defending the Gulf:
    A Survey".

Eliot, Theodore L., Jr. (1979) "Afghanistan After
    the 1978 Revolution". Strategic Review
    7: 57-62.

El-Khawas, Mohammed A. and Cohen, Barry. (eds.)
    (1976) The Kissinger Study of Southern
    Africa. Westport, Conn.: Lawrence Hill & Co.

Eran, Oded. (1979) "The Soviet Perception of
    Influence: the Case of the Middle East 1973-
    1976". In Yaacov Ro'i (ed.) The Limits to
    Power: Soviet Policy in the Middle East.
    New York: St. Martin's.

Erikson, John. (1976) "Detente: Soviet Policy and
    Purpose". Strategic Review 4: 37-44.

Evron, Yair. (1979) "Great Powers' Military Interven-
    tion in the Middle East". In Milton
    Leitenberg and Gabriel Sheffer (eds.) Great
    Power Intervention in the Middle East. Oxford:
    Pergamon Press.

Falk, Richard. (1980) "The Menace of the New Cycle
    of Interventionary Diplomacy". Journal of
    Peace Research 17: 201-206.

Farer, T.J. (1974) "Regulation of Foreign Interven-
    tion in Civil Armed Conflict". Recueil des
    Cours 142: 291-406.

_____. (1979) War Clouds Over the Horn of Africa.
    (2nd ed.) New York: Carnegie Endowment for
    International Peace.

Franck, T.M. and Weisband, E. (1970) "The Johnson and
    Brezhnev Doctrines". Stanford Law Review
    22: 979-1013.

Franck, T.M. and Weisband, E. (1971) Word Politics:
    Verbal Strategy Among the Superpowers. New
    York: Oxford University Press.

Friedmann, Wolfgang. (1970) "Intervention and Inter-
    national Law" in Jaquet.

Garrity, Patrick J. (1980) "The Soviet Military
    Stake in Afghanistan: 1956-1979". R.U.S.I.
    125: 31-37.

Girling, J.L.S. (1980) America and the Third World:
    Revolution and Intervention. London: Routledge
    and Kegan Paul.

Gonzalez, Edward. (1977) "Complexities of Cuban
    Foreign Policy". Problems of Communism
    no. 6: 3.

Gurtov, Melvin. (1974) The United States Against the
    Third World: Antinationalism and Interven-
    tion. New York: Praeger.

Hagen, Lawrence S. (1979) "Detente Derailed: the
    Dilemmas of a Misbegotten Concept". Millenium:
    Journal of International Studies 8: 67-72.

Hallett, Richard. (1979) "The South African Inter-
    vention in Angola, 1975-76". African Affairs
    77: 347-386.

Hart, H.L.A. (1961) The Concept of Law. Oxford:
    Clarendon Press.

Hassner, Pierre. (1977) "Super-Power Rivalries,
    Conflicts and Co-operation". The Diffusion of
    Power II: Conflict and its Control. Adelphi
    Papers no. 134. London: I.I.S.S.

Himes, Joseph S. (1980) Conflict and Conflict Manage-
    ment. Athens: University of Georgia Press.

Holbraad, Carsten. (1979) *Superpowers and International Conflict*. New York: St. Martin's.

House. see U.S. Congress. House.

Howard, Michael. (ed.) (1979) *Restraints on War*. Oxford: Oxford University Press.

Hull, Galen. (1977) "Internationalizing the Shaba Conflict". *Africa Report* 22 (no. 4): 4-9.

_____. (1979) "The French Connection in Africa: Zaire and South Africa". *Journal of Southern African Studies* 5: 220-233.

Jaquet, Louis G.M. (1970) *Intervention in International Politics*. The Hague: Netherlands Institute of International Affairs.

Kahler, Miles. (1979) "Rumours of War: the 1914 Analogy". *Foreign Affairs* 58: 374-396.

Kapcia, A.M. (1979) "Cuba's African Involvement: A New Perspective". *Survey* no. 107: 142-159.

Kaplan, Stephen S. (1981) *Diplomacy of Power: Soviet Armed Forces as a Political Instrument*. Washington: The Brookings Institute.

Karenin, A. (1975) "Detente and New Variations of Old Doctrines". *International Affairs* no. 6: 98-106.

Kaufman, A.S. (1979) "The Modern Revolutionary Democracy and National-Liberation Revolutions". *Rabochiy Klass I Sovremennyy Mir* no. 6: 68-79 (*J.P.R.S.* 75252).

Khalilzad, Zalmy. (1980) "Afghanistan and the Crisis in American Foreign Policy". *Survival* 22: 151-160.

Kim, G. (1980) "Social Development and Ideological Struggle in the Developing Countries". International Affairs (Moscow) no. 4: 63-75.

Kissinger, H. (1975) "Statement before the Senate Foreign Relations Committee". Survival 17: 35-49.

_____. (1976) "The 1976 Alastair Buchan Memorial Lecture". Survival 18: 194-203.

_____. (1979) White House Years. Boston: Little, Brown & Co.

Klinghoffer, Arthur J. (1980) The Angolan War: A Study in Soviet Foreign Policy in the Third World. Boulder, Co.: Westview Press.

Kosukhin, N.D. (1979) "Scientific Socialism in the Ideological and Political Life of African Nations". Rabochiy Klass I Sovremennyy Mir no. 6: 129-138 (J.P.R.S. 75252).

Kubalkova, V. and Cruickshank, A.A. (1978) "The Soviet Concept of Peaceful Coexistence: Some Theoretical and Semantic Problems". Australian Journal of Politics and History 24: 184-198.

_____. (1980) Marxism-Leninism and The Theory of International Relations. London: Routledge and Kegan Paul.

_____. (1981) "Marxist Perspectives and the Study of International Relations: a Rejoinder". Review of International Studies 7: 51-57.

Lange, Peer H. (1981) "Afghanistan: World Politics Without Sensitivity". Aussenpolitik 32: 73-85.

Larrabee, Stephen. (1976) "Moscow, Angola and the Dialectics of Detente". World Today 32: 173-182.

Lauterpacht, H. (1947) "The International Protection of Human Rights". Recueil des Cours 70: 19-23.

Legum, Colin. (1976) "The Soviet Union, China and the West in Southern Africa". Foreign Affairs 54: 745-762.

_____. (1980) "Foreign Intervention in Africa I". Year Book of World Affairs 1980. London: Stevens and Sons.

_____. (1981) "Foreign Intervention in Africa II". Year Book of World Affairs 1981. London: Stevens and Sons.

Legum, Colin and Hodges, Tony. (1978) After Angola: the War over Southern Africa. New York: Africana Publishing.

Legvold, Robert. (1979) "The Super-Rivals: Conflict in the Third World". Foreign Affairs 57: 755-778.

Little, Richard. (1975) Intervention: External Involvement in Civil Wars. London: Martin Robertson.

Lowenthal, Abraham F. (1977) "Cuba's Africa Adventure". International Security 2: 3-10.

Luard, Evan. (1972) The International Regulation of Civil War. London: Thames & Hudson.

McConnell, James M. (1979) "The 'Rules of the Game': A Theory of the Practice of Superpower Naval Diplomacy". In Bradford Dismukes and James M. McConnell (eds.) Soviet Naval Diplomacy. New York: Pergamon Press.

McConnell, James M. and Dismukes, Bradford. (1979) "Soviet Diplomacy of Force in the Third World". Problems of Communism 28 (no. 1): 26.

Manchka, P.I. (1976) "On the Theory of Revolutionary Democracy". Voprosy istorii K.P.S.S. no. 10: 57-69.

Mangold, Peter. (1979) "Shaba I and Shaba II". Survival 21: 107-115.

Manin, Aleth. (1978) "L'Intervention française au Shaba (19 mai-14 juin 1978)". Annuaire Français de Droit International 24: 159-188.

Manning, Robert. (1977) "Zaire Crisis: Challenge for Mobutu". New African 11: 382-383.

Marcum, John A. (1978) The Angolan Revolution Vol. 2: Exile Politics and Guerrilla Warfare (1962-1976). Cambridge, Mass.: M.I.T. Press.

Meissner, Boris. (1980) "Soviet Foreign Policy and Afghanistan". Aussenpolitik 31 (no. 3): 260-282.

Miller, J.D.B. (1970) "Unlimited Competition or Spheres of Responsibility". Soviet-American Relations and World Order. Adelphi Paper no. 66. London: I.I.S.S.

Miller, Linda B. (1977) "Superpower Conflict in the 1980s". Millenium: Journal of International Studies 6: 58-62.

Mitchell, R.J. (1978) "The New Brezhnev Doctrine". World Politics 30: 374-390.

Mitchell, R. Judson and Leonhard, Alan T. (1976) "Changing Soviet Attitudes Toward International Law: An Incorporative Approach". Georgia Journal of International and Comparative Law 6: 227-244.

Modelski, George A. (1961) The International Relations of Internal War. Princeton: Centre of International Studies. Woodrow Wilson School of Public and International Affairs.

Moore, John Norton. (ed.) (1974) Law and Civil War in
    the Modern World. Baltimore: John Hopkins
    University Press.

Nekrasov, N. "1980: Survey of International Life".
    Kommunist no. 18 (Dec. 1980): 115-131 (J.P.R.S.
    77731).

New York Times.

Newell, Richard S. (1981)   "International Responses
    to the Afghanistan Crisis". World Today 37:
    172-181.

O'Brien, William V. (1979) U.S. Military Intervention:
    Law and Morality. The Washington Papers
    no. 68. Beverly Hills, Ca.: Sage Publications.

Ottaway, Marina and Ottaway, David. (1978) Ethiopia:
    Empire in Revolution. New York: Africana
    Publishing.

Papp, Daniel S. (1977)   "National Liberation during
    Detente: the Soviet Outlook". International
    Journal 32: 82-89.

Pavlov, O. (1968)   "Proletarian Internationalism and
    Defense of Socialist Gains". International
    Affairs (Moscow) no. 10: 10-14.

Petrov, Vladimir. (1975) U.S.-Soviet Detente: Past,
    Present and Future. Washington: American
    Enterprise Institute.

Ponomarev, B. "Joint Struggle of the Workers and
    National-Liberation Movements Against
    Imperialism and for Social Progress".
    Kommunist no. 16 (Nov. 1980): 31-47.

Roberts, James W. (1977)   "Lenin's Theory of
    Imperialism in Soviet Usage". Soviet Studies
    29: 353-372.

Rosenau, James. (1968) "The Concept of Intervention". Journal of International Affairs 22: 165-176.

Samuels, Michael A. et al. (1979) Implications of Soviet and Cuban Activities in Africa for U.S. Policy. Washington: Center for Strategic and International Studies, Georgetown University.

Sanakoyev, Sh. (1980) "Proletarian Internationalism: a Decisive Factor of Peace and Social Progress". International Affairs (Moscow) no. 6: 81-91.

Schachter, Oscar. (1968) "Toward a Theory of International Obligation". Virginia Journal of International Law 8: 300-322.

_____. (1977) "The Twilight Existence of Non-Binding International Agreements". American Journal of International Law 71: 296-304.

Schwarz, Urs. (1970) "Intervention: the Historical Development II" in Jaquet.

Schwarzenberger, George. (1959) "Hegemonial Intervention". Year Book of World Affairs 1959. London: Stevens & Sons.

_____. (1981) "Detente and International Law". Year Book of World Affairs 1981. London: Stevens & Sons.

Schwebel, Stephen M. (1974) "Wars of Liberation - as Fought in U.N. Organs" in Moore.

Selassie, Bereket Habte. (1980) Conflict and Intervention in the Horn of Africa. New York: Monthly Review Press.

Sella, Amnon. (1981) Soviet Political and Military Conduct in the Middle East. London: Macmillan.

Semyonov, Y. (1980) "Peking and the National Liberation Movement". International Affairs (Moscow) no. 1: 29-39.

Senate. see U.S. Congress. Senate.

Sidenko, V. (1980) "The Leninist Foreign Policy Course and the National Liberation Movement". Mirovaya Ekonomika I Mezhdunarodnyye Otnosheniya no. 2: 3-18 (J.P.R.S. 75730).

Simes, Dimitri K. (1977) Detente and Conflict: Soviet Foreign Policy 1972-1977. The Washington Papers no. 44. Beverly Hills, Ca.: Sage Publications.

_____. (1980) "The Death of Detente?" International Security 5: 3-25.

Sonnenfeldt, Helmut. (1980) "Implications of the Soviet Invasion of Afghanistan for East-West Relations". Atlantic Community Quarterly 18: 184-192.

Stassen, J.C. (1977) "Intervention in Internal Wars: Traditional Norms and Contemporary Trends". South African Yearbook of International Law 3: 65-84.

Strategic Survey (1975-1981). London: I.I.S.S.

Tarabrin, E. (1979) "Africa in a New Round of the Liberation Struggle". Survival 21: 172-175.

Thiele, Terry Vernon. (1978) "Norms of Intervention in a Decolonized World". New York University Journal of International Law and Politics 11: 141-174.

Thomas, Ann Van Wynen and Thomas, A.J. (1956) Non-Intervention. Dallas: Southern Methodist University Press.

Toman, Jiri. (1975) "La Conception soviétique des guerres de libération nationale". In Antonio Cassese (ed.) Current Problems of International Law. Milan: Dott. A. Guifrè Editore.

U.N. (1976) Monthly Chronicle 13 no. 4.

U.N. (1980) Monthly Chronicle 17 no. 2.

U.S. Congress. House. (1976) Disaster Assistance in Angola. Hearings before the Subcommittee on International Resources, Food and Energy of the Committee on International Relations. November 5, 1975, February 26, 1976, March 10, 1976.

_____. (1977) Foreign Assistance Legislation for Fiscal Year 1978. Hearings before the Subcommittee on Africa of the Committee on International Relations. March 17, 18, 23, 28, 29 and April 28, 1977.

_____. (1978a) Impact of Cuban-Soviet Ties in the Western Hemisphere. Hearings before the Subcommittee on Inter-American Affairs of the Committee on International Relations. March 15, 1978.

_____. (1978b) Congressional Oversight of War Powers Compliance: Zaire Airlift. Hearings before the Subcommittee on African Affairs of the Committee on Foreign Affairs. October 16, 1979.

_____. (1979a) Crisis in the Subcontinent: Afghanistan and Pakistan. Hearings before the Subcommittee on Asian and Pacific Affairs of the Committee on Foreign Affairs. May 15 and September 26, 1979.

U.S. Congress. House. (1979b) <u>U.S. Interests in</u>
<u>Africa.</u> Hearings before the Subcommittee on
African Affairs of the Committee on Foreign
Affairs. October 16, 1979.

_____. (1980) <u>East-West Relations in the Aftermath</u>
<u>of the Soviet Invasion of Afghanistan.</u>
Hearings before the Subcommittee on Europe and
the Middle East of the Committee on Foreign
Affairs. January 24, 30, 1980.

U.S. Congress. Senate. (1975) <u>Security Supporting</u>
<u>Assistance for Zaire.</u> Hearings before the
Subcommittees on African Affairs and on
Foreign Assistance of the Committee on Foreign
Relations. October 24, 1975.

_____. (1976a) <u>Angola.</u> Hearings before the
Subcommittee on African Affairs of the
Committee on Foreign Relations. January 29,
February 3, 4, 6, 1976.

_____. (1976b) <u>Foreign Policy Choices for the</u>
<u>Seventies and Eighties.</u> Hearings before the
Committee on Foreign Affairs. March 16, 1976.

_____. (1976c) <u>Ethiopia and the Horn of Africa.</u>
Hearings before the Subcommittee on African
Affairs of the Committee on Foreign Relations.
August 4, 5, 6, 1976.

_____. (1978) <u>U.S. Policy Toward Africa.</u> Hearings
before the Subcommittee on African Affairs of
the Committee on Foreign Relations. May 12,
1978.

U.S. Department of State. (1968) <u>U.S. Statement on</u>
<u>Spheres of Influence.</u> Press Release no. 190,
August 23, 1968.

_____. (1972-1980) <u>Bulletin 61-80.</u>

U.S. Department of State. (1975) <u>Digest of United States Practice in International Law 1974</u>.

U.S. Office of the President. (1970) <u>U.S. Foreign Policy for the 1970s: A New Strategy for Peace. A Report by President Richard Nixon to the Congress</u>. February 18, 1970.

_____. (1971) <u>U.S. Foreign Policy for the 1970s: Building for Peace. A Report to the Congress by Richard Nixon, President of the United States</u>. February 25, 1971.

_____. (1972) <u>U.S. Foreign Policy for the 1970s: The Emerging Structure of Peace. A Report to the Congress by Richard Nixon, President of the United States</u>. February 9, 1972.

_____. (1973) <u>U.S. Foreign Policy for the 1970s: Shaping a Durable Peace. A Report to the Congress by Richard Nixon, President of the United States</u>. May 3, 1973.

Valenta, Jiri. (1978) "The Soviet-Cuban Intervention in Angola, 1975". <u>Studies in Comparative Communism</u> 11: 3-33.

_____. (1980a) "The Soviet Invasion of Afghanistan: the Difficulty of Knowing Where to Stop". <u>Orbis</u> 24: 201-218.

_____. (1980b) "From Prague to Kabul: the Soviet Style of Invasion". <u>International Security</u> 5: 114-141.

_____. (1981) "The Soviet-Cuban Alliance in Africa and the Carribbean". <u>World Today</u> 37: 45-53.

Vazquez, Modesto Seara. (1973) "Zones of Influence". <u>Year Book of World Affairs 1973</u>. London: Stevens & Sons.

Vigor, P.H. (1975) The Soviet View of War, Peace and Neutrality. London: Routledge and Kegan Paul.

Vincent, R.J. (1974) Nonintervention and International Order. Princeton: Princeton University Press.

Walzer, Michael. (1977) Just and Unjust Wars. New York: Basic Books.

Weissman, Stephen. (1978) "The C.I.A. and U.S. Policy in Zaire and Angola". In René Lemarchand (ed.) American Policy in Southern Africa: the Stakes and the Stance. Washington: University Press of America.

Weltman, John J. (1979) "Detente and the Decline of Geography". Jerusalem Journal of International Affairs 4 no. 2: 75-94.

Wessel, Nils H. (1979) "Soviet Views of Multipolarity and the Emerging Balance of Power". Orbis 22: 785-814.

Whetton, Lawrence. (1978) "The Soviet-Cuban Presence in the Horn of Africa". R.U.S.I. 123: 39-45.

Young, Lawrence. (1978) "Zaire: the Unending Crisis". Foreign Affairs 57: 164-185.

Young, Oran R. (1968) "Intervention and International Systems". Journal of International Affairs 22: 177-187.

Younger, Kenneth G. (1970) "Intervention: the Historical Development I" in Jaquet.

Zagoria, Donald S. (1979) "Into the Breach: New Soviet Alliances in the Third World". Foreign Affairs 57: 733-754.

Zartmann, William. (1975) "Negotiations: Theory and Reality". Journal of International Affairs 29: 69-77.

ABOUT THE AUTHOR

Neil Matheson, a native of Montreal, was educated at St. John's College, Oxford and received his M.A. in International Affairs from Carleton University, Ottawa. An earlier version of this paper was submitted in partial fulfilment of that degree's requirements. He is currently Public Affairs Analyst with Alcan Aluminium Limited, Montreal.

DATE DUE

GAYLORD

PRINTED IN U.S.A